ATS-145   ADMISSION TEST SERIES

This is your
PASSBOOK for...

Certified and Registered Central Service Technician (CRCST)

Test Preparation Study Guide
Questions & Answers

COPYRIGHT NOTICE

This book is SOLELY intended for, is sold ONLY to, and its use is RESTRICTED to individual, bona fide applicants or candidates who qualify by virtue of having seriously filed applications for appropriate license, certificate, professional and/or promotional advancement, higher school matriculation, scholarship, or other legitimate requirements of education and/or governmental authorities.

This book is NOT intended for use, class instruction, tutoring, training, duplication, copying, reprinting, excerption, or adaptation, etc., by:

1) Other publishers
2) Proprietors and/or Instructors of "Coaching" and/or Preparatory Courses
3) Personnel and/or Training Divisions of commercial, industrial, and governmental organizations
4) Schools, colleges, or universities and/or their departments and staffs, including teachers and other personnel
5) Testing Agencies or Bureaus
6) Study groups which seek by the purchase of a single volume to copy and/or duplicate and/or adapt this material for use by the group as a whole without having purchased individual volumes for each of the members of the group
7) Et al.

Such persons would be in violation of appropriate Federal and State statutes.

PROVISION OF LICENSING AGREEMENTS – Recognized educational, commercial, industrial, and governmental institutions and organizations, and others legitimately engaged in educational pursuits, including training, testing, and measurement activities, may address request for a licensing agreement to the copyright owners, who will determine whether, and under what conditions, including fees and charges, the materials in this book may be used them. In other words, a licensing facility exists for the legitimate use of the material in this book on other than an individual basis. However, it is asseverated and affirmed here that the material in this book CANNOT be used without the receipt of the express permission of such a licensing agreement from the Publishers. Inquiries re licensing should be addressed to the company, attention rights and permissions department.

All rights reserved, including the right of reproduction in whole or in part, in any form or by any means, electronic or mechanical, including photocopying, recording, or by any information storage and retrieval system, without permission in writing from the Publisher.

Copyright © 2024 by
National Learning Corporation

212 Michael Drive, Syosset, NY 11791
(516) 921-8888 • www.passbooks.com
E-mail: info@passbooks.com

PUBLISHED IN THE UNITED STATES OF AMERICA

PASSBOOK® SERIES

THE *PASSBOOK® SERIES* has been created to prepare applicants and candidates for the ultimate academic battlefield – the examination room.

At some time in our lives, each and every one of us may be required to take an examination – for validation, matriculation, admission, qualification, registration, certification, or licensure.

Based on the assumption that every applicant or candidate has met the basic formal educational standards, has taken the required number of courses, and read the necessary texts, the *PASSBOOK® SERIES* furnishes the one special preparation which may assure passing with confidence, instead of failing with insecurity. Examination questions – together with answers – are furnished as the basic vehicle for study so that the mysteries of the examination and its compounding difficulties may be eliminated or diminished by a sure method.

This book is meant to help you pass your examination provided that you qualify and are serious in your objective.

The entire field is reviewed through the huge store of content information which is succinctly presented through a provocative and challenging approach – the question-and-answer method.

A climate of success is established by furnishing the correct answers at the end of each test.

You soon learn to recognize types of questions, forms of questions, and patterns of questioning. You may even begin to anticipate expected outcomes.

You perceive that many questions are repeated or adapted so that you can gain acute insights, which may enable you to score many sure points.

You learn how to confront new questions, or types of questions, and to attack them confidently and work out the correct answers.

You note objectives and emphases, and recognize pitfalls and dangers, so that you may make positive educational adjustments.

Moreover, you are kept fully informed in relation to new concepts, methods, practices, and directions in the field.

You discover that you are actually taking the examination all the time: you are preparing for the examination by "taking" an examination, not by reading extraneous and/or supererogatory textbooks.

In short, this PASSBOOK®, used directedly, should be an important factor in helping you to pass your test.

CERTIFIED AND REGISTERED CENTRAL SERVICE TECHNICIAN (CRCST)

The exam will test your knowledge of the following 7 areas:
1. **Cleaning, Decontamination, and Disinfection**
2. **Preparation and Packaging**
3. **Sterilization Process**
4. **Patient Care Equipment**
5. **Sterile Storage and Inventory Management**
6. **Documentation and Record Maintenance**
7. **Customer Relations**

The Content Outline was created through the job task analysis and details the specific areas of knowledge necessary to perform the duties of a Central Service Technician. The Content Outline also details the percentage weight for each of the 7 sections. The higher the percentage weight, the more heavily the questions in that area will affect your overall test score.

1. **Cleaning, Decontamination, and Disinfection** [Percentage Weight: 20%]
    a. **Safety Standards**
        i. OSHA/Blood Borne Pathogens
        ii. Microbiology (e.g. cross contamination, microbial transmission, chain of infection)
        iii. Where to obtain information
        iv. Body Mechanics
        v. Sharp Safety
        vi. Equipment Operation
        vii. Where to find MSDS
        viii. Location and Operation of eyewash station
        ix. Location and Operation of shower
        x. Ergonomics (e.g. work-flow)
        xi. Chemical Safety
        xii. Traffic flow
        xiii. How to contain, transport, and receive soiled items into decontamination or soiled utility rooms

    b. **Personal Protective Equipment (PPE)**
        i. What PPE to put on
        ii. How to put PPE on
        iii. How to take PPE off
        iv. When to change PPE
        v. How to dispose of PPE
        vi. Hand-washing
        vii. How to contain, transport, and receive soiled items into decontamination or soiled utility rooms

    c. **Temperature and Humidity of the Work Environment**
        i. Standards for temperature
        ii. Standards for humidity
        iii. How to record
        iv. Frequency to record
        v. What to do if not within the parameters

d. Preparing Work Area For Decontamination
  i. Correct cleaning agent or chemicals for cleaning process
  ii. Supplies Needed (e.g. brush, towels)
  iii. Equipment (e.g. compressed air, water)
  iv. How to mix chemicals following the manufacturer's instructions For Use (IFU) (e.g.dilution)
  v. How to check and replenish chemicals in equipment
  vi. How to properly dispose of chemicals
  vii. How to determine the correct chemicals for the equipment

e. Quality Tests
  i. Efficacy testing process for washers
  ii. Efficacy testing process for ultrasonic
  iii. Efficacy testing process for Automated Endoscope Reprocessor (AER)
  iv. Efficacy testing process for cart washer
  v. Water quality test process
  vi. When to test
  vii. How to interpret tests

f. Troubleshooting Cleaning Equipment
  i. Who to call if malfunction or have a question
  ii. How to identify and respond to alarms
  iii. How to clean strainers/drains
  iv. Water pressure
  v. Location of outlets: on/off, regular, and emergency
  vi. Chemical feed line processes
  vii. How to clean and test spray arms
  viii. How to check manifolds and baskets
  ix. Operator's manual (where to find, how to use)
  x. How to close equipment doors and proper operation of doors

g. Disposable Items from Non-Disposable Items
  i. Difference between disposable and non-disposable items (e.g. single-use versus re-useable, laparoscopic tips)
  ii. Third-party vendor items (e.g. identification of items to return to third-party vendors)
  iii. Disposable and non-disposable linens
  iv. Process of broken and repairable instrumentation
  v. How to dispose of sharps and non-reprocessed items (e.g. biohazards versus non-regulated trash, sharps container)

h. Preparing Items for Decontamination
  i. How to disassemble instrument
  ii. Manual and mechanical cleaning according to IFU
  iii. Where the IFU is located
  iv. Methods for reducing the risk of Toxic Anterior Segment Syndrome (TASS)
  v. How to load items into the equipment
  vi. How to clean strainer/drains
  vii. Special precautions for Creutzfeldt-Jacob Disease (CJD) instruments

i. **Cleaning and Decontaminating Non-Disposable Items**
    i. Location of IFU
    ii. Proper opening and positioning of instruments
    iii. Operation times for processes (e.g. manual and mechanical)
    iv. Operation of light and magnification devices
    v. When and how to use water and air
    vi. What goes in each sink (e.g. two or three sink method)
    vii. Soak process
    viii. Selection of correct brush and size
    ix. Brush care
    x. Prevention of aerosols
    xi. Proper loading of equipment

j. **Selecting Appropriate Disinfectant**
    i. How to mix and test chemicals
    ii. Three levels of Spaulding Classification (e.g. non-critical, semi-critical, critical)
    iii. Documentation of chemical testing
    iv. Disinfectant family (what they do, how to use)

k. **Disinfecting Instruments and Equipment**
    i. Use of correct disinfectant
    ii. Exposure times
    iii. Rinsing

l. **Transferring Items to Preparation Area**
    i. Air exchange (e.g. negative pressure, positive pressure)
    ii. How to perform visual check for cleanliness

2. **Preparation and Packaging** [*Percentage Weight: 20%*]

    a. **Temperature and Humidity of the Work Environment**
        i. Standards for Temperature
        ii. Standards for humidity
        iii. How to record
        iv. Frequency to record
        v. What to do if not within the parameters

    b. **Preparing Work Area for Packaging**
        i. Supplies needed
        ii. Dress code
        iii. Work area requirements (e.g. cleaning requirements)
        iv. Location of IFUs

    c. **Receiving Items for Preparation**
        i. Item identification (e.g. visual, computerized)
        ii. How to unload equipment
        iii. How to unload equipment How to check for cleanliness
        iv. How to sort items (e.g. service, facility, loaner)
        v. How to accept items through pass-through window

d. **Inspecting Items for Cleanliness and Functionality**
    i. How to check for cleanliness and functionality
    ii. How to follow the IFU
    iii. Proper testing tools and process for checking functionality of items (e.g. sharpness testing)
    iv. How to assemble, test, and disassemble items according to IFUs
    v. How to remove and replace unacceptable items
    vi. How to lubricate items according to IFUs

e. **Selecting Items for Assembly**
    i. How to obtain the appropriate count sheets, peel pack list, tray list (e.g. where to place count sheets)
    ii. How to read and identify items (e.g. books, product number, computers, tape, etching)
    iii. How to cross-reference different instruments
    iv. How to size and measure items
    v. Visual identification and proper names of common instruments

f. **Assembling Items for Packaging**
    i. Proper handling procedures
    ii. Instrument protection devices (e.g. tip protectors, foam, mats)
    iii. Tray liners
    iv. Proper instrument placement (e.g. facilitate sterilization, protect instruments)
    v. Instrument organizers
    vi. Classes and appropriate use of chemical indicators (e.g. proper placement, intended cycle)
    vii. Weight limits and weight distribution

g. **Packaging Method**
    i. How to select appropriate packaging method (e.g. size, packaging weight)
    ii. Packaging Method (e.g. flat wrap, peel pack, container)
    iii. Sterilization method/cycle to be used
    iv. External indicators
    v. Tamper evident seals
    vi. Proper application method of packaging
    vii. Proper wrapping technique

h. **Labeling Method**
    i. Importance of legible handwriting
    ii. Approved writing instrument
    iii. Placement of labeling and writing (e.g. write on plastic side of peel pouch, write on tape not wrapper)
    iv. How to identify trays missing items
    v. Correct tray information
    vi. Technician identification
    vii. Storage destination
    viii. Special information identifiers (e.g. implant, loaners, sterilization methods/cycle)
    ix. Date of sterilization/date of expiration (e.g. event-related versus time)

i. **Transferring Items to Appropriate Area**
    i. Location of sterilization areas (e.g. low temperature, high temperature)
    ii. Location of staging area
    iii. How to prioritize for rapid turn-around
    iv. How to handle items without damaging (e.g. stacking, rough handling)
    v. Delivery locations
    vi. Air exchanges (e.g. negative pressure, positive pressure)
    vii. Body mechanics
    viii. Ergonomics
    ix. How to track items (e.g. manual, computer)
    x. Traffic flow

3. **Sterilization Process** [Percentage Weight: 20%]

    a. **Temperature and Humidity of the Work Environment**
        i. Standards for Temperature
        ii. Standards for humidity
        iii. How to record
        iv. Frequency to record
        v. What to do if not within the parameters

    b. **Preparing Work Area for Sterilization**
        i. Supplies needed (e.g. printer supplies, test packs, label gun supplies)
        ii. Perform sterilizer component checks according to manufacturer's IFU
        iii. Perform cleaning according to manufacturer's IFU

    c. **Sterilizer Tests**
        i. Leak tests
        ii. Bowie Dick/air removal test according to standard
        iii. Placement of biological test packs for sterilization
        iv. When to perform test (e.g. repair, construction, malfunction, routine)

    d. **Receiving Items for Sterilization**
        i. id How to move items from cart to cart
        ii. Proper body mechanics
        iii. Proper handling of item to preserve packaging integrity
        iv. How to access IFUs

    e. **Sterilization Method and Cycle**
        i. Functionality of sterilizer
        ii. How to select and change the cycle
        iii. How to identify appropriate use of external indicators (e.g. sterilization method, placement)
        iv. Sterilization method of items
        v. Identification of appropriate packaging for the sterilization method

    f. **Pre-Sterilization Package Integrity**
        i. What comprises integrity (e.g. holes, filters, broken locks and seals)
        ii. Filter placement, locks, seals, and external indicators

g. **Loading Sterilizer**
    i. Metal mass versus load configuration
    ii. Wrapped versus rigid containers and peel pouch
    iii. Biological tests
    iv. Appropriate placement of items

h. **Operating and Monitoring Sterilization Equipment**
    i. How to replace and dispose of empty cartridges/tanks /cassettes
    ii. How to select cycle
    iii. Where to place biological or air removal tests
    iv. Temperature requirements for each sterilization method
    v. How to access IFUs

i. **Cycle Parameters**
    i. How to interpret printout (e.g. temperature, time, and pressure exposure)
    ii. Sign-off procedures to ensure accountability

j. **Unloading Sterilizer**
    i. What maintains sterility (e.g. Cooling time, temperature, handling)
    ii. Body mechanics
    iii. Ergonomics
    iv. Traffic flow
    v. Proper PPE

k. **Post-Sterilization Package Integrity**
    i. What compromises integrity (e.g. holes, filters, broken locks and seals, moisture)
    ii. Filter placement, locks, seals, and external indicators

l. **Test Results**
    i. Proper handling and incubation of the biological test
    ii. How to interpret test results

m. **Potential Process Failures**
    i. How to identify a process failure (e.g. wet packs, color change, failure to meet sterilization parameters)
    ii. Procedure for follow-up after process failure

n. **Lot Control Number**
    i. How to produce a lot control number
    ii. Where to apply lot control number according to manufacturer's IFU

o. **Documenting Sterilization Load Contents**
    i. How to identify load contents
    ii. How and where to record (e.g. computer, manual)

p. **Transferring Sterilized Items to Storage and Distribution**
    i. Location of storage areas
    ii. Location of staging area
    iii. How to prioritize for rapid turn-around
    iv. How to handle items without damaging (e.g. stacking, rough handling)
    v. Air exchanges (e.g. negative pressure, positive pressure)
    vi. Body mechanics

vii. Ergonomics
viii. How to track items (e.g. manual, computer)
ix. Traffic flow
x. Early release of implantable devices

4. Patient Care Equipment [Percentage Weight: 10%]

a. Temperature and Humidity of the Work Environment
i. Standards for Temperature
ii. Standards for humidity
iii. How to record
iv. Frequency to record
v. What to do if not within the parameters

b. Preparing Work Area for Distribution
i. Supplies needed
ii. Dress code
iii. Location of IFUs

c. Receiving Items for Preparation
i. Process for recording and tracking rental equipment
ii. Item identification (e.g. visual, computerized)
iii. How to unload equipment
iv. How to sort items (e.g. type of equipment)

d. Inspecting Equipment for Cleanliness and Functionality
i. 'How to check for cleanliness
ii. How to check for compliance with safety standards (e.g. frayed cords, preventative maintenance date, damage)

e. Assembling Equipment for Distribution
i. How to assemble equipment for distribution
ii. How to test equipment per manufacturer's use policy
iii. How to package equipment
iv. How to label equipment
v. How to access IFUs
vi. How to access disposable components

f. Care and Handling
i. What equipment requires charging or battery replacement
ii. Location and proper storage of equipment
iii. Environmental requirements for stored equipment (e.g. dry, clean)
iv. Preventative maintenance dates

g. Distributing Equipment
i. Process for recording
ii. Types of equipment maintained in CSSD
iii. Delivery protocols
iv. Delivery locations (e.g. OR, ED, Labor and Delivery)

h. Tracking Medical Equipment
i. Systems used (e.g. manual, computer, RFID, hybrid)
ii. How to record and track the distribution

i. **Repair and Safety Inspection**
      iii. Process for completing biomedical work order (e.g. manual, computerized)
      iv. How to identify label for safety inspection/preventative maintenance

5. **Sterile Storage and Inventory Management** [Percentage Weight: 10%]

   a. **Temperature and Humidity of the Work Environment**
      i. Standards for temperature
      ii. Standards for humidity
      iii. How to record
      iv. Frequency to record
      v. What to do if not within the parameters

   b. **Preparing Work Area for Sterile Storage**
      i. Supplies needed
      ii. Dress code
      iii. Work area requirements (e.g. cleaning requirements)
      iv. Location of IFUs

   c. **Ordering Inventory**
      i. The ordering process (e.g. par levels, computerized, manual)
      ii. How to identify the product (e.g., catalog numbers, item number, descriptions)
      iii. Unit of measure (e.g. each, box, package, case)
      iv. How to handle back-orders

   d. **Receiving and Inspecting Inventory**
      i. What compromises integrity (e.g. holes, filters, broken locks and seals, water damage, dust)
      ii. External indicators and expiration dates
      iii. How to match delivery document to what was received (e.g. signing for deliveries)

   e. **Stocking and Rotating Inventory**
      i. Location of supplies
      ii. Shelf life policy (e.g. First In First Out (FIFO), expiration, event-related)
      iii. Process for rotating inventory
      iv. Proper storage requirements
      v. Proper break-out area (e.g. corrugated cardboard, external shipping containers)

   f. **Distributing Sterile and Non-Sterile Items**
      i. Distribution methods
      ii. Proper handling of items
      iii. Ergonomics
      iv. Body mechanics
      v. Transport guidelines (e.g. closed cart, bins, dustcovers)

   g. **Monitoring Item Usage**
      i. What system to use (e.g. manual, computerized)
      ii. Identification of items

h. Tracking Items Distributed by CSSD
  i. High dollar items
  ii. Specialty carts
  iii. Critical items
  iv. Vendor-owned items
  v. How items are tracked (e.g. manual, RFID, computerized)
  vi. When to review MSDS information and how to access and interpret MSDS information

i. Disposing Inventory
  i. How to handle recalled items
  ii. Open/not used single use item
  iii. Damaged items
  iv. Expired items
  v. Obsolete items
  vi. Recycled items
  vii. Donations of items to others

6. Documentation and Record Maintenance [Percentage Weight: 10%]

a. Record Maintenance
  i. Environmental conditions for records storage
  ii. Protocol of time-frame to keep records
  iii. What needs to be kept
  iv. Where kept (on-site, off-site)
  v. How to retrieve

b. Temperature, Humidity, and Corrective Action
  i. Acceptable temperature humidity ranges for work areas
  ii. Procedure for reporting deficiency

c. Quality Test Results
  i. Ultrasonic systems
  ii. Water quality and temperature
  iii. Bowie Dicks tests (e.g. run as first load of the day, empty load)
  iv. Sterilizer leak tests (e.g. when test should be performed)
  v. Biological and chemical tests (e.g. lot numbers, running control tests, correct placement of tests, incubation procedure, how to interpret results, recall process in case of undesirable outcomes)
  vi. How to interpret the results of the test
  vii. Take corrective action if test fails
  viii. Washer decontamination process (e.g. frequency, type)
  ix. Cart washer

d. High Level Disinfection (HLD) Process
  i. Safety measures when using HLD
  ii. Proper disposal methods
  iii. Dilution labeling requirements (e.g. concentration, expiration, end of use date)
  iv. Technician information
  v. Patient information

e. **Employee Incident Reports**
      i. Hospital reporting policy
      ii. Exposure control plan
      iii. State and federal safety regulations
      iv. Risk management and safety management policies
      v. Patient tracing procedure (e.g. in event of needle stick, cut)

7. **Customer Relations** [Percentage Weight: 10%]

   a. **Customer Requests**
      i. Phone Etiquette
      ii. Active listening (e.g. technique of repeating back to customer "I heard you say")

   b. **Communication**
      i. Decision-making skills
      ii. Communication method (email, face-to-face, phone)
      iii. Medical terminology (e.g. anatomy and physiology, surgical terminology, instrumentation)

   c. **Internal and External Teams**
      i. Troubleshooting task forces
      ii. Types of teams (e.g. quality, cross disciplinary) Engagement level (e.g. attendance, follow-through)
      iii. Completion of assignments
      iv. Role on the team (e.g. leader, observer)

   d. **Facility and Procedures**
      i. Where to find policies and procedures
      ii. How to interpret policies and procedures
      iii. Frequency of review
      iv. Responsibility related to review (e.g. make suggestions, keep current with them)

HOW TO TAKE A TEST

I. YOU MUST PASS AN EXAMINATION

A. *WHAT EVERY CANDIDATE SHOULD KNOW*

Examination applicants often ask us for help in preparing for the written test. What can I study in advance? What kinds of questions will be asked? How will the test be given? How will the papers be graded?

As an applicant for a civil service examination, you may be wondering about some of these things. Our purpose here is to suggest effective methods of advance study and to describe civil service examinations.

Your chances for success on this examination can be increased if you know how to prepare. Those "pre-examination jitters" can be reduced if you know what to expect. You can even experience an adventure in good citizenship if you know why civil service exams are given.

B. *WHY ARE CIVIL SERVICE EXAMINATIONS GIVEN?*

Civil service examinations are important to you in two ways. As a citizen, you want public jobs filled by employees who know how to do their work. As a job seeker, you want a fair chance to compete for that job on an equal footing with other candidates. The best-known means of accomplishing this two-fold goal is the competitive examination.

Exams are widely publicized throughout the nation. They may be administered for jobs in federal, state, city, municipal, town or village governments or agencies.

Any citizen may apply, with some limitations, such as the age or residence of applicants. Your experience and education may be reviewed to see whether you meet the requirements for the particular examination. When these requirements exist, they are reasonable and applied consistently to all applicants. Thus, a competitive examination may cause you some uneasiness now, but it is your privilege and safeguard.

C. *HOW ARE CIVIL SERVICE EXAMS DEVELOPED?*

Examinations are carefully written by trained technicians who are specialists in the field known as "psychological measurement," in consultation with recognized authorities in the field of work that the test will cover. These experts recommend the subject matter areas or skills to be tested; only those knowledges or skills important to your success on the job are included. The most reliable books and source materials available are used as references. Together, the experts and technicians judge the difficulty level of the questions.

Test technicians know how to phrase questions so that the problem is clearly stated. Their ethics do not permit "trick" or "catch" questions. Questions may have been tried out on sample groups, or subjected to statistical analysis, to determine their usefulness.

Written tests are often used in combination with performance tests, ratings of training and experience, and oral interviews. All of these measures combine to form the best-known means of finding the right person for the right job.

II. HOW TO PASS THE WRITTEN TEST

A. NATURE OF THE EXAMINATION

To prepare intelligently for civil service examinations, you should know how they differ from school examinations you have taken. In school you were assigned certain definite pages to read or subjects to cover. The examination questions were quite detailed and usually emphasized memory. Civil service exams, on the other hand, try to discover your present ability to perform the duties of a position, plus your potentiality to learn these duties. In other words, a civil service exam attempts to predict how successful you will be. Questions cover such a broad area that they cannot be as minute and detailed as school exam questions.

In the public service similar kinds of work, or positions, are grouped together in one "class." This process is known as *position-classification*. All the positions in a class are paid according to the salary range for that class. One class title covers all of these positions, and they are all tested by the same examination.

B. FOUR BASIC STEPS

1) Study the announcement

How, then, can you know what subjects to study? Our best answer is: "Learn as much as possible about the class of positions for which you've applied." The exam will test the knowledge, skills and abilities needed to do the work.

Your most valuable source of information about the position you want is the official exam announcement. This announcement lists the training and experience qualifications. Check these standards and apply only if you come reasonably close to meeting them.

The brief description of the position in the examination announcement offers some clues to the subjects which will be tested. Think about the job itself. Review the duties in your mind. Can you perform them, or are there some in which you are rusty? Fill in the blank spots in your preparation.

Many jurisdictions preview the written test in the exam announcement by including a section called "Knowledge and Abilities Required," "Scope of the Examination," or some similar heading. Here you will find out specifically what fields will be tested.

2) Review your own background

Once you learn in general what the position is all about, and what you need to know to do the work, ask yourself which subjects you already know fairly well and which need improvement. You may wonder whether to concentrate on improving your strong areas or on building some background in your fields of weakness. When the announcement has specified "some knowledge" or "considerable knowledge," or has used adjectives like "beginning principles of..." or "advanced ... methods," you can get a clue as to the number and difficulty of questions to be asked in any given field. More questions, and hence broader coverage, would be included for those subjects which are more important in the work. Now weigh your strengths and weaknesses against the job requirements and prepare accordingly.

3) Determine the level of the position

Another way to tell how intensively you should prepare is to understand the level of the job for which you are applying. Is it the entering level? In other words, is this the position in which beginners in a field of work are hired? Or is it an intermediate or advanced level? Sometimes this is indicated by such words as "Junior" or "Senior" in the class title. Other jurisdictions use Roman numerals to designate the level – Clerk I, Clerk II, for example. The word "Supervisor" sometimes appears in the title. If the level is not indicated by the title, check the description of duties. Will you be working under very close supervision, or will you have responsibility for independent decisions in this work?

4) Choose appropriate study materials

Now that you know the subjects to be examined and the relative amount of each subject to be covered, you can choose suitable study materials. For beginning level jobs, or even advanced ones, if you have a pronounced weakness in some aspect of your training, read a modern, standard textbook in that field. Be sure it is up to date and has general coverage. Such books are normally available at your library, and the librarian will be glad to help you locate one. For entry-level positions, questions of appropriate difficulty are chosen – neither highly advanced questions, nor those too simple. Such questions require careful thought but not advanced training.

If the position for which you are applying is technical or advanced, you will read more advanced, specialized material. If you are already familiar with the basic principles of your field, elementary textbooks would waste your time. Concentrate on advanced textbooks and technical periodicals. Think through the concepts and review difficult problems in your field.

These are all general sources. You can get more ideas on your own initiative, following these leads. For example, training manuals and publications of the government agency which employs workers in your field can be useful, particularly for technical and professional positions. A letter or visit to the government department involved may result in more specific study suggestions, and certainly will provide you with a more definite idea of the exact nature of the position you are seeking.

III. KINDS OF TESTS

Tests are used for purposes other than measuring knowledge and ability to perform specified duties. For some positions, it is equally important to test ability to make adjustments to new situations or to profit from training. In others, basic mental abilities not dependent on information are essential. Questions which test these things may not appear as pertinent to the duties of the position as those which test for knowledge and information. Yet they are often highly important parts of a fair examination. For very general questions, it is almost impossible to help you direct your study efforts. What we can do is to point out some of the more common of these general abilities needed in public service positions and describe some typical questions.

1) General information

Broad, general information has been found useful for predicting job success in some kinds of work. This is tested in a variety of ways, from vocabulary lists to questions about current events. Basic background in some field of work, such as sociology or economics, may be sampled in a group of questions. Often these are principles which have become familiar to most persons through exposure rather than through formal training. It is difficult to advise you how to study for these questions; being alert to the world around you is our best suggestion.

2) Verbal ability

An example of an ability needed in many positions is verbal or language ability. Verbal ability is, in brief, the ability to use and understand words. Vocabulary and grammar tests are typical measures of this ability. Reading comprehension or paragraph interpretation questions are common in many kinds of civil service tests. You are given a paragraph of written material and asked to find its central meaning.

3) Numerical ability

Number skills can be tested by the familiar arithmetic problem, by checking paired lists of numbers to see which are alike and which are different, or by interpreting charts and graphs. In the latter test, a graph may be printed in the test booklet which you are asked to use as the basis for answering questions.

4) Observation

A popular test for law-enforcement positions is the observation test. A picture is shown to you for several minutes, then taken away. Questions about the picture test your ability to observe both details and larger elements.

5) Following directions

In many positions in the public service, the employee must be able to carry out written instructions dependably and accurately. You may be given a chart with several columns, each column listing a variety of information. The questions require you to carry out directions involving the information given in the chart.

6) Skills and aptitudes

Performance tests effectively measure some manual skills and aptitudes. When the skill is one in which you are trained, such as typing or shorthand, you can practice. These tests are often very much like those given in business school or high school courses. For many of the other skills and aptitudes, however, no short-time preparation can be made. Skills and abilities natural to you or that you have developed throughout your lifetime are being tested.

Many of the general questions just described provide all the data needed to answer the questions and ask you to use your reasoning ability to find the answers. Your best preparation for these tests, as well as for tests of facts and ideas, is to be at your physical and mental best. You, no doubt, have your own methods of getting into an exam-taking mood and keeping "in shape." The next section lists some ideas on this subject.

IV. KINDS OF QUESTIONS

Only rarely is the "essay" question, which you answer in narrative form, used in civil service tests. Civil service tests are usually of the short-answer type. Full instructions for answering these questions will be given to you at the examination. But in case this is your first experience with short-answer questions and separate answer sheets, here is what you need to know:

1) Multiple-choice Questions

Most popular of the short-answer questions is the "multiple choice" or "best answer" question. It can be used, for example, to test for factual knowledge, ability to solve problems or judgment in meeting situations found at work.

A multiple-choice question is normally one of three types—
- It can begin with an incomplete statement followed by several possible endings. You are to find the one ending which *best* completes the statement, although some of the others may not be entirely wrong.
- It can also be a complete statement in the form of a question which is answered by choosing one of the statements listed.

- It can be in the form of a problem – again you select the best answer.

Here is an example of a multiple-choice question with a discussion which should give you some clues as to the method for choosing the right answer:

When an employee has a complaint about his assignment, the action which will *best* help him overcome his difficulty is to
   A. discuss his difficulty with his coworkers
   B. take the problem to the head of the organization
   C. take the problem to the person who gave him the assignment
   D. say nothing to anyone about his complaint

In answering this question, you should study each of the choices to find which is best. Consider choice "A" – Certainly an employee may discuss his complaint with fellow employees, but no change or improvement can result, and the complaint remains unresolved. Choice "B" is a poor choice since the head of the organization probably does not know what assignment you have been given, and taking your problem to him is known as "going over the head" of the supervisor. The supervisor, or person who made the assignment, is the person who can clarify it or correct any injustice. Choice "C" is, therefore, correct. To say nothing, as in choice "D," is unwise. Supervisors have and interest in knowing the problems employees are facing, and the employee is seeking a solution to his problem.

2) True/False Questions

The "true/false" or "right/wrong" form of question is sometimes used. Here a complete statement is given. Your job is to decide whether the statement is right or wrong.

SAMPLE: A roaming cell-phone call to a nearby city costs less than a non-roaming call to a distant city.

This statement is wrong, or false, since roaming calls are more expensive.

This is not a complete list of all possible question forms, although most of the others are variations of these common types. You will always get complete directions for answering questions. Be sure you understand *how* to mark your answers – ask questions until you do.

V. RECORDING YOUR ANSWERS

Computer terminals are used more and more today for many different kinds of exams.

For an examination with very few applicants, you may be told to record your answers in the test booklet itself. Separate answer sheets are much more common. If this separate answer sheet is to be scored by machine – and this is often the case – it is highly important that you mark your answers correctly in order to get credit.

An electronic scoring machine is often used in civil service offices because of the speed with which papers can be scored. Machine-scored answer sheets must be marked with a pencil, which will be given to you. This pencil has a high graphite content which responds to the electronic scoring machine. As a matter of fact, stray dots may register as answers, so do not let your pencil rest on the answer sheet while you are pondering the correct answer. Also, if your pencil lead breaks or is otherwise defective, ask for another.

Since the answer sheet will be dropped in a slot in the scoring machine, be careful not to bend the corners or get the paper crumpled.

The answer sheet normally has five vertical columns of numbers, with 30 numbers to a column. These numbers correspond to the question numbers in your test booklet. After each number, going across the page are four or five pairs of dotted lines. These short dotted lines have small letters or numbers above them. The first two pairs may also have a "T" or "F" above the letters. This indicates that the first two pairs only are to be used if the questions are of the true-false type. If the questions are multiple choice, disregard the "T" and "F" and pay attention only to the small letters or numbers.

Answer your questions in the manner of the sample that follows:

32. The largest city in the United States is
    A. Washington, D.C.
    B. New York City
    C. Chicago
    D. Detroit
    E. San Francisco

1) Choose the answer you think is best. (New York City is the largest, so "B" is correct.)
2) Find the row of dotted lines numbered the same as the question you are answering. (Find row number 32)
3) Find the pair of dotted lines corresponding to the answer. (Find the pair of lines under the mark "B.")
4) Make a solid black mark between the dotted lines.

VI. BEFORE THE TEST

Common sense will help you find procedures to follow to get ready for an examination. Too many of us, however, overlook these sensible measures. Indeed, nervousness and fatigue have been found to be the most serious reasons why applicants fail to do their best on civil service tests. Here is a list of reminders:

- Begin your preparation early – Don't wait until the last minute to go scurrying around for books and materials or to find out what the position is all about.
- Prepare continuously – An hour a night for a week is better than an all-night cram session. This has been definitely established. What is more, a night a week for a month will return better dividends than crowding your study into a shorter period of time.
- Locate the place of the exam – You have been sent a notice telling you when and where to report for the examination. If the location is in a different town or otherwise unfamiliar to you, it would be well to inquire the best route and learn something about the building.
- Relax the night before the test – Allow your mind to rest. Do not study at all that night. Plan some mild recreation or diversion; then go to bed early and get a good night's sleep.
- Get up early enough to make a leisurely trip to the place for the test – This way unforeseen events, traffic snarls, unfamiliar buildings, etc. will not upset you.
- Dress comfortably – A written test is not a fashion show. You will be known by number and not by name, so wear something comfortable.

- Leave excess paraphernalia at home – Shopping bags and odd bundles will get in your way. You need bring only the items mentioned in the official notice you received; usually everything you need is provided. Do not bring reference books to the exam. They will only confuse those last minutes and be taken away from you when in the test room.
- Arrive somewhat ahead of time – If because of transportation schedules you must get there very early, bring a newspaper or magazine to take your mind off yourself while waiting.
- Locate the examination room – When you have found the proper room, you will be directed to the seat or part of the room where you will sit. Sometimes you are given a sheet of instructions to read while you are waiting. Do not fill out any forms until you are told to do so; just read them and be prepared.
- Relax and prepare to listen to the instructions
- If you have any physical problem that may keep you from doing your best, be sure to tell the test administrator. If you are sick or in poor health, you really cannot do your best on the exam. You can come back and take the test some other time.

VII. AT THE TEST

The day of the test is here and you have the test booklet in your hand. The temptation to get going is very strong. Caution! There is more to success than knowing the right answers. You must know how to identify your papers and understand variations in the type of short-answer question used in this particular examination. Follow these suggestions for maximum results from your efforts:

1) Cooperate with the monitor

The test administrator has a duty to create a situation in which you can be as much at ease as possible. He will give instructions, tell you when to begin, check to see that you are marking your answer sheet correctly, and so on. He is not there to guard you, although he will see that your competitors do not take unfair advantage. He wants to help you do your best.

2) Listen to all instructions

Don't jump the gun! Wait until you understand all directions. In most civil service tests you get more time than you need to answer the questions. So don't be in a hurry. Read each word of instructions until you clearly understand the meaning. Study the examples, listen to all announcements and follow directions. Ask questions if you do not understand what to do.

3) Identify your papers

Civil service exams are usually identified by number only. You will be assigned a number; you must not put your name on your test papers. Be sure to copy your number correctly. Since more than one exam may be given, copy your exact examination title.

4) Plan your time

Unless you are told that a test is a "speed" or "rate of work" test, speed itself is usually not important. Time enough to answer all the questions will be provided, but this does not mean that you have all day. An overall time limit has been set. Divide the total time (in minutes) by the number of questions to determine the approximate time you have for each question.

5) Do not linger over difficult questions

If you come across a difficult question, mark it with a paper clip (useful to have along) and come back to it when you have been through the booklet. One caution if you do this – be sure to skip a number on your answer sheet as well. Check often to be sure that you have not lost your place and that you are marking in the row numbered the same as the question you are answering.

6) Read the questions

Be sure you know what the question asks! Many capable people are unsuccessful because they failed to *read* the questions correctly.

7) Answer all questions

Unless you have been instructed that a penalty will be deducted for incorrect answers, it is better to guess than to omit a question.

8) Speed tests

It is often better NOT to guess on speed tests. It has been found that on timed tests people are tempted to spend the last few seconds before time is called in marking answers at random – without even reading them – in the hope of picking up a few extra points. To discourage this practice, the instructions may warn you that your score will be "corrected" for guessing. That is, a penalty will be applied. The incorrect answers will be deducted from the correct ones, or some other penalty formula will be used.

9) Review your answers

If you finish before time is called, go back to the questions you guessed or omitted to give them further thought. Review other answers if you have time.

10) Return your test materials

If you are ready to leave before others have finished or time is called, take ALL your materials to the monitor and leave quietly. Never take any test material with you. The monitor can discover whose papers are not complete, and taking a test booklet may be grounds for disqualification.

VIII. EXAMINATION TECHNIQUES

1) Read the general instructions carefully. These are usually printed on the first page of the exam booklet. As a rule, these instructions refer to the timing of the examination; the fact that you should not start work until the signal and must stop work at a signal, etc. If there are any *special* instructions, such as a choice of questions to be answered, make sure that you note this instruction carefully.

2) When you are ready to start work on the examination, that is as soon as the signal has been given, read the instructions to each question booklet, underline any key words or phrases, such as *least, best, outline, describe* and the like. In this way you will tend to answer as requested rather than discover on reviewing your paper that you *listed without describing*, that you selected the *worst* choice rather than the *best* choice, etc.

3) If the examination is of the objective or multiple-choice type – that is, each question will also give a series of possible answers: A, B, C or D, and you are called upon to select the best answer and write the letter next to that answer on your answer paper – it is advisable to start answering each question in turn. There may be anywhere from 50 to 100 such questions in the three or four hours allotted and you can see how much time would be taken if you read through all the questions before beginning to answer any. Furthermore, if you come across a question or group of questions which you know would be difficult to answer, it would undoubtedly affect your handling of all the other questions.

4) If the examination is of the essay type and contains but a few questions, it is a moot point as to whether you should read all the questions before starting to answer any one. Of course, if you are given a choice – say five out of seven and the like – then it is essential to read all the questions so you can eliminate the two that are most difficult. If, however, you are asked to answer all the questions, there may be danger in trying to answer the easiest one first because you may find that you will spend too much time on it. The best technique is to answer the first question, then proceed to the second, etc.

5) Time your answers. Before the exam begins, write down the time it started, then add the time allowed for the examination and write down the time it must be completed, then divide the time available somewhat as follows:
    - If 3-1/2 hours are allowed, that would be 210 minutes. If you have 80 objective-type questions, that would be an average of 2-1/2 minutes per question. Allow yourself no more than 2 minutes per question, or a total of 160 minutes, which will permit about 50 minutes to review.
    - If for the time allotment of 210 minutes there are 7 essay questions to answer, that would average about 30 minutes a question. Give yourself only 25 minutes per question so that you have about 35 minutes to review.

6) The most important instruction is to *read each question* and make sure you know what is wanted. The second most important instruction is to *time yourself properly* so that you answer every question. The third most important instruction is to *answer every question*. Guess if you have to but include something for each question. Remember that you will receive no credit for a blank and will probably receive some credit if you write something in answer to an essay question. If you guess a letter – say "B" for a multiple-choice question – you may have guessed right. If you leave a blank as an answer to a multiple-choice question, the examiners may respect your feelings but it will not add a point to your score. Some exams may penalize you for wrong answers, so in such cases *only*, you may not want to guess unless you have some basis for your answer.

7) Suggestions
    a. Objective-type questions
        1. Examine the question booklet for proper sequence of pages and questions
        2. Read all instructions carefully
        3. Skip any question which seems too difficult; return to it after all other questions have been answered
        4. Apportion your time properly; do not spend too much time on any single question or group of questions

5. Note and underline key words – *all, most, fewest, least, best, worst, same, opposite,* etc.
6. Pay particular attention to negatives
7. Note unusual option, e.g., unduly long, short, complex, different or similar in content to the body of the question
8. Observe the use of "hedging" words – *probably, may, most likely,* etc.
9. Make sure that your answer is put next to the same number as the question
10. Do not second-guess unless you have good reason to believe the second answer is definitely more correct
11. Cross out original answer if you decide another answer is more accurate; do not erase until you are ready to hand your paper in
12. Answer all questions; guess unless instructed otherwise
13. Leave time for review

   b. Essay questions
      1. Read each question carefully
      2. Determine exactly what is wanted. Underline key words or phrases.
      3. Decide on outline or paragraph answer
      4. Include many different points and elements unless asked to develop any one or two points or elements
      5. Show impartiality by giving pros and cons unless directed to select one side only
      6. Make and write down any assumptions you find necessary to answer the questions
      7. Watch your English, grammar, punctuation and choice of words
      8. Time your answers; don't crowd material

8) Answering the essay question

Most essay questions can be answered by framing the specific response around several key words or ideas. Here are a few such key words or ideas:

M's: manpower, materials, methods, money, management
P's: purpose, program, policy, plan, procedure, practice, problems, pitfalls, personnel, public relations

   a. Six basic steps in handling problems:
      1. Preliminary plan and background development
      2. Collect information, data and facts
      3. Analyze and interpret information, data and facts
      4. Analyze and develop solutions as well as make recommendations
      5. Prepare report and sell recommendations
      6. Install recommendations and follow up effectiveness

   b. Pitfalls to avoid
      1. *Taking things for granted* – A statement of the situation does not necessarily imply that each of the elements is necessarily true; for example, a complaint may be invalid and biased so that all that can be taken for granted is that a complaint has been registered

2. *Considering only one side of a situation* – Wherever possible, indicate several alternatives and then point out the reasons you selected the best one
3. *Failing to indicate follow up* – Whenever your answer indicates action on your part, make certain that you will take proper follow-up action to see how successful your recommendations, procedures or actions turn out to be
4. *Taking too long in answering any single question* – Remember to time your answers properly

IX. AFTER THE TEST

Scoring procedures differ in detail among civil service jurisdictions although the general principles are the same. Whether the papers are hand-scored or graded by machine we have described, they are nearly always graded by number. That is, the person who marks the paper knows only the number – never the name – of the applicant. Not until all the papers have been graded will they be matched with names. If other tests, such as training and experience or oral interview ratings have been given, scores will be combined. Different parts of the examination usually have different weights. For example, the written test might count 60 percent of the final grade, and a rating of training and experience 40 percent. In many jurisdictions, veterans will have a certain number of points added to their grades.

After the final grade has been determined, the names are placed in grade order and an eligible list is established. There are various methods for resolving ties between those who get the same final grade – probably the most common is to place first the name of the person whose application was received first. Job offers are made from the eligible list in the order the names appear on it. You will be notified of your grade and your rank as soon as all these computations have been made. This will be done as rapidly as possible.

People who are found to meet the requirements in the announcement are called "eligibles." Their names are put on a list of eligible candidates. An eligible's chances of getting a job depend on how high he stands on this list and how fast agencies are filling jobs from the list.

When a job is to be filled from a list of eligibles, the agency asks for the names of people on the list of eligibles for that job. When the civil service commission receives this request, it sends to the agency the names of the three people highest on this list. Or, if the job to be filled has specialized requirements, the office sends the agency the names of the top three persons who meet these requirements from the general list.

The appointing officer makes a choice from among the three people whose names were sent to him. If the selected person accepts the appointment, the names of the others are put back on the list to be considered for future openings.

That is the rule in hiring from all kinds of eligible lists, whether they are for typist, carpenter, chemist, or something else. For every vacancy, the appointing officer has his choice of any one of the top three eligibles on the list. This explains why the person whose name is on top of the list sometimes does not get an appointment when some of the persons lower on the list do. If the appointing officer chooses the second or third eligible, the No. 1 eligible does not get a job at once, but stays on the list until he is appointed or the list is terminated.

X. HOW TO PASS THE INTERVIEW TEST

The examination for which you applied requires an oral interview test. You have already taken the written test and you are now being called for the interview test – the final part of the formal examination.

You may think that it is not possible to prepare for an interview test and that there are no procedures to follow during an interview. Our purpose is to point out some things you can do in advance that will help you and some good rules to follow and pitfalls to avoid while you are being interviewed.

What is an interview supposed to test?

The written examination is designed to test the technical knowledge and competence of the candidate; the oral is designed to evaluate intangible qualities, not readily measured otherwise, and to establish a list showing the relative fitness of each candidate – as measured against his competitors – for the position sought. Scoring is not on the basis of "right" and "wrong," but on a sliding scale of values ranging from "not passable" to "outstanding." As a matter of fact, it is possible to achieve a relatively low score without a single "incorrect" answer because of evident weakness in the qualities being measured.

Occasionally, an examination may consist entirely of an oral test – either an individual or a group oral. In such cases, information is sought concerning the technical knowledges and abilities of the candidate, since there has been no written examination for this purpose. More commonly, however, an oral test is used to supplement a written examination.

Who conducts interviews?

The composition of oral boards varies among different jurisdictions. In nearly all, a representative of the personnel department serves as chairman. One of the members of the board may be a representative of the department in which the candidate would work. In some cases, "outside experts" are used, and, frequently, a businessman or some other representative of the general public is asked to serve. Labor and management or other special groups may be represented. The aim is to secure the services of experts in the appropriate field.

However the board is composed, it is a good idea (and not at all improper or unethical) to ascertain in advance of the interview who the members are and what groups they represent. When you are introduced to them, you will have some idea of their backgrounds and interests, and at least you will not stutter and stammer over their names.

What should be done before the interview?

While knowledge about the board members is useful and takes some of the surprise element out of the interview, there is other preparation which is more substantive. It *is* possible to prepare for an oral interview – in several ways:

1) Keep a copy of your application and review it carefully before the interview

This may be the only document before the oral board, and the starting point of the interview. Know what education and experience you have listed there, and the sequence and dates of all of it. Sometimes the board will ask you to review the highlights of your experience for them; you should not have to hem and haw doing it.

2) Study the class specification and the examination announcement

Usually, the oral board has one or both of these to guide them. The qualities, characteristics or knowledges required by the position sought are stated in these documents. They offer valuable clues as to the nature of the oral interview. For example, if the job involves supervisory responsibilities, the announcement will usually indicate that knowledge of modern supervisory methods and the qualifications of the candidate as a supervisor will be tested. If so, you can expect such questions, frequently in the form of a hypothetical situation which you are expected to solve. NEVER go into an oral without knowledge of the duties and responsibilities of the job you seek.

3) Think through each qualification required

Try to visualize the kind of questions you would ask if you were a board member. How well could you answer them? Try especially to appraise your own knowledge and background in each area, *measured against the job sought*, and identify any areas in which you are weak. Be critical and realistic – do not flatter yourself.

4) Do some general reading in areas in which you feel you may be weak

For example, if the job involves supervision and your past experience has NOT, some general reading in supervisory methods and practices, particularly in the field of human relations, might be useful. Do NOT study agency procedures or detailed manuals. The oral board will be testing your understanding and capacity, not your memory.

5) Get a good night's sleep and watch your general health and mental attitude

You will want a clear head at the interview. Take care of a cold or any other minor ailment, and of course, no hangovers.

What should be done on the day of the interview?

Now comes the day of the interview itself. Give yourself plenty of time to get there. Plan to arrive somewhat ahead of the scheduled time, particularly if your appointment is in the fore part of the day. If a previous candidate fails to appear, the board might be ready for you a bit early. By early afternoon an oral board is almost invariably behind schedule if there are many candidates, and you may have to wait. Take along a book or magazine to read, or your application to review, but leave any extraneous material in the waiting room when you go in for your interview. In any event, relax and compose yourself.

The matter of dress is important. The board is forming impressions about you – from your experience, your manners, your attitude, and your appearance. Give your personal appearance careful attention. Dress your best, but not your flashiest. Choose conservative, appropriate clothing, and be sure it is immaculate. This is a business interview, and your appearance should indicate that you regard it as such. Besides, being well groomed and properly dressed will help boost your confidence.

Sooner or later, someone will call your name and escort you into the interview room. *This is it.* From here on you are on your own. It is too late for any more preparation. But remember, you asked for this opportunity to prove your fitness, and you are here because your request was granted.

What happens when you go in?

The usual sequence of events will be as follows: The clerk (who is often the board stenographer) will introduce you to the chairman of the oral board, who will introduce you to the other members of the board. Acknowledge the introductions before you sit down. Do not be surprised if you find a microphone facing you or a stenotypist sitting by. Oral interviews are usually recorded in the event of an appeal or other review.

Usually the chairman of the board will open the interview by reviewing the highlights of your education and work experience from your application – primarily for the benefit of the other members of the board, as well as to get the material into the record. Do not interrupt or comment unless there is an error or significant misinterpretation; if that is the case, do not hesitate. But do not quibble about insignificant matters. Also, he will usually ask you some question about your education, experience or your present job – partly to get you to start talking and to establish the interviewing "rapport." He may start the actual questioning, or turn it over to one of the other members. Frequently, each member undertakes the questioning on a particular area, one in which he is perhaps most competent, so you can expect each member to participate in the examination. Because time is limited, you may also expect some rather abrupt switches in the direction the questioning takes, so do not be upset by it. Normally, a board member will not pursue a single line of questioning unless he discovers a particular strength or weakness.

After each member has participated, the chairman will usually ask whether any member has any further questions, then will ask you if you have anything you wish to add. Unless you are expecting this question, it may floor you. Worse, it may start you off on an extended, extemporaneous speech. The board is not usually seeking more information. The question is principally to offer you a last opportunity to present further qualifications or to indicate that you have nothing to add. So, if you feel that a significant qualification or characteristic has been overlooked, it is proper to point it out in a sentence or so. Do not compliment the board on the thoroughness of their examination – they have been sketchy, and you know it. If you wish, merely say, "No thank you, I have nothing further to add." This is a point where you can "talk yourself out" of a good impression or fail to present an important bit of information. Remember, *you close the interview yourself*.

The chairman will then say, "That is all, Mr. _____, thank you." Do not be startled; the interview is over, and quicker than you think. Thank him, gather your belongings and take your leave. Save your sigh of relief for the other side of the door.

How to put your best foot forward

Throughout this entire process, you may feel that the board individually and collectively is trying to pierce your defenses, seek out your hidden weaknesses and embarrass and confuse you. Actually, this is not true. They are obliged to make an appraisal of your qualifications for the job you are seeking, and they want to see you in your best light. Remember, they must interview all candidates and a non-cooperative candidate may become a failure in spite of their best efforts to bring out his qualifications. Here are 15 suggestions that will help you:

1) Be natural – Keep your attitude confident, not cocky

If you are not confident that you can do the job, do not expect the board to be. Do not apologize for your weaknesses, try to bring out your strong points. The board is interested in a positive, not negative, presentation. Cockiness will antagonize any board member and make him wonder if you are covering up a weakness by a false show of strength.

2) Get comfortable, but don't lounge or sprawl

Sit erectly but not stiffly. A careless posture may lead the board to conclude that you are careless in other things, or at least that you are not impressed by the importance of the occasion. Either conclusion is natural, even if incorrect. Do not fuss with your clothing, a pencil or an ashtray. Your hands may occasionally be useful to emphasize a point; do not let them become a point of distraction.

3) Do not wisecrack or make small talk

This is a serious situation, and your attitude should show that you consider it as such. Further, the time of the board is limited – they do not want to waste it, and neither should you.

4) Do not exaggerate your experience or abilities
In the first place, from information in the application or other interviews and sources, the board may know more about you than you think. Secondly, you probably will not get away with it. An experienced board is rather adept at spotting such a situation, so do not take the chance.

5) If you know a board member, do not make a point of it, yet do not hide it
Certainly you are not fooling him, and probably not the other members of the board. Do not try to take advantage of your acquaintanceship – it will probably do you little good.

6) Do not dominate the interview
Let the board do that. They will give you the clues – do not assume that you have to do all the talking. Realize that the board has a number of questions to ask you, and do not try to take up all the interview time by showing off your extensive knowledge of the answer to the first one.

7) Be attentive
You only have 20 minutes or so, and you should keep your attention at its sharpest throughout. When a member is addressing a problem or question to you, give him your undivided attention. Address your reply principally to him, but do not exclude the other board members.

8) Do not interrupt
A board member may be stating a problem for you to analyze. He will ask you a question when the time comes. Let him state the problem, and wait for the question.

9) Make sure you understand the question
Do not try to answer until you are sure what the question is. If it is not clear, restate it in your own words or ask the board member to clarify it for you. However, do not haggle about minor elements.

10) Reply promptly but not hastily
A common entry on oral board rating sheets is "candidate responded readily," or "candidate hesitated in replies." Respond as promptly and quickly as you can, but do not jump to a hasty, ill-considered answer.

11) Do not be peremptory in your answers
A brief answer is proper – but do not fire your answer back. That is a losing game from your point of view. The board member can probably ask questions much faster than you can answer them.

12) Do not try to create the answer you think the board member wants
He is interested in what kind of mind you have and how it works – not in playing games. Furthermore, he can usually spot this practice and will actually grade you down on it.

13) Do not switch sides in your reply merely to agree with a board member
Frequently, a member will take a contrary position merely to draw you out and to see if you are willing and able to defend your point of view. Do not start a debate, yet do not surrender a good position. If a position is worth taking, it is worth defending.

14) Do not be afraid to admit an error in judgment if you are shown to be wrong

The board knows that you are forced to reply without any opportunity for careful consideration. Your answer may be demonstrably wrong. If so, admit it and get on with the interview.

15) Do not dwell at length on your present job

The opening question may relate to your present assignment. Answer the question but do not go into an extended discussion. You are being examined for a *new* job, not your present one. As a matter of fact, try to phrase ALL your answers in terms of the job for which you are being examined.

Basis of Rating

Probably you will forget most of these "do's" and "don'ts" when you walk into the oral interview room. Even remembering them all will not ensure you a passing grade. Perhaps you did not have the qualifications in the first place. But remembering them will help you to put your best foot forward, without treading on the toes of the board members.

Rumor and popular opinion to the contrary notwithstanding, an oral board wants you to make the best appearance possible. They know you are under pressure – but they also want to see how you respond to it as a guide to what your reaction would be under the pressures of the job you seek. They will be influenced by the degree of poise you display, the personal traits you show and the manner in which you respond.

ABOUT THIS BOOK

This book contains tests divided into Examination Sections. Go through each test, answering every question in the margin. We have also attached a sample answer sheet at the back of the book that can be removed and used. At the end of each test look at the answer key and check your answers. On the ones you got wrong, look at the right answer choice and learn. Do not fill in the answers first. Do not memorize the questions and answers, but understand the answer and principles involved. On your test, the questions will likely be different from the samples. Questions are changed and new ones added. If you understand these past questions you should have success with any changes that arise. Tests may consist of several types of questions. We have additional books on each subject should more study be advisable or necessary for you. Finally, the more you study, the better prepared you will be. This book is intended to be the last thing you study before you walk into the examination room. Prior study of relevant texts is also recommended. NLC publishes some of these in our Fundamental Series. Knowledge and good sense are important factors in passing your exam. Good luck also helps. So now study this Passbook, absorb the material contained within and take that knowledge into the examination. Then do your best to pass that exam.

EXAMINATION SECTION

EXAMINATION SECTION
TEST 1

DIRECTIONS: Each question or incomplete statement is followed by several suggested answers or completions. Select the one that BEST answers the question or completes the statement. *PRINT THE LETTER OF THE CORRECT ANSWER IN THE SPACE AT THE RIGHT.*

1. _____ disinfection uses heat to kill all microorganisms with the exception of spores.
   A. Ultraviolet   B. Ultrasonic   C. Thermal   D. Ozone

   1._____

2. What type of solution inhibits the growth of bacteria and is typically used topically only on animate objects?
   A. Antiseptic   B. Disinfectant   C. Bactericide   D. Fungicide

   2._____

3. _____ are often pathogenic to humans because they grow best at body temperature.
   A. Extremophiles
   B. Thermophiles
   C. Mesophiles
   D. Psyhchrophiles

   3._____

4. What technique should be used for brushing instruments?
   A. Brushing should be done under water
   B. Brushing should be done above water
   C. Brushing against the grain of the device
   D. Brushing should be performed only with wire brushes

   4._____

5. The final rinse water used for cleaning should be treated through which of the following systems?
   A. Water conductivity
   B. Sanitation
   C. Deionization
   D. Sterilization

   5._____

6. Which product is used to kill microorganisms?
   A. Detergents
   B. Germicidal detergents
   C. Soaps
   D. Enzyme Presoaks

   6._____

7. _____ in water can be removed by water softeners.
   A. Iron and Chloride
   B. Calcium and Magnesium
   C. Iron and Pyrogens
   D. Silicates and Pyrogens

   7._____

8. The ideal chloride concentration for tap water is _____ ppm or less.
   A. 50   B. 100   C. 150   D. 200

   8._____

9. Water purification is normally performed through the use of which of the following?
   A. Pre-filter
   B. Post-filter
   C. Pre-filter or Post-filter
   D. Pre-filter and Post-filter

   9._____

10. Turbid water has what kind of appearance?
    A. Clear   B. Particulate   C. Cloudy   D. Soapy

11. When should the process of pre-cleaning be initiated?
    A. Prior to items being sorted
    B. Immediately after instruments are inspected
    C. Upon receipt of the devices in the Central Services Area
    D. Immediately upon completion of an invasive procedure

12. The ideal silicate level in water used for cleaning is _____ ppm or less.
    A. 50   B. 100   C. 150   D. 200

13. Which process requires the use of deionized water?
    A. Rapid infusions   B. Sterile irrigation
    C. Steam sterilization   D. Heating/cooling therapy units

14. Which type of water impurity will result in bluish or rainbow-like stains?
    A. Calcium   B. Fluoride
    C. Chlorides and Solids   D. Iron and Silicates

15. Which of the following is the primary purpose for using manual cleaners?
    A. Removing soil
    B. Killing microorganisms
    C. Reducing the cost associated with cleaning
    D. Should only be used if automated cleaning equipment is malfunctioning

16. For what is multi-enzymatic cleaning products containing lipase useful for cleaning?
    A. Sugars   B. Fats   C. Starches   D. Proteins

17. What is the appropriate pH for purified water?
    A. 4.5 - 5.5   B. 5.5 - 6.5   C. 6.5 - 7.5   D. 7.5 - 8.5

18. Entoxins, pyrogens, and bacteria can be removed from water using which process?
    A. Reverse osmosis   B. Aeration
    C. Electronic purification   D. Dissolved oxygen generation

19. Which of the following can be classified as regulated medical waste?
    A. Discarded sterilization wraps
    B. Blood-soaked sponges
    C. General trash from the operating room
    D. Spent copier toner cartridges

20. Which of the following are commonly used to break down fatty tissue on instruments?
    A. Amylase enzymes   B. Lipase enzymes
    C. Protease enzymes   D. Neutral pH cleaners

21. All of the following is accurate regarding the use of mechanical washers EXCEPT
    A. Trays with lids should be opened
    B. Multi-level trays should be separated
    C. Instruments should be disassembled and opened
    D. All items should be washed on the same cycle

22. For what reason should the water be degassed each time the tank of an ultrasonic cleaner is changed?
    Excess bubbles
    A. from the filling process reduce the energy of the cavitation process
    B. decrease the temperature of the tank
    C. make it difficult to see the items being cleaned
    D. reduce the effectiveness of the detergent

23. Specialized clothing or equipment worn by an employee for protection against biological hazards is referred to as
    A. personal protective equipment
    B. hazard equipment
    C. restricted apparel
    D. safety apparel

24. What is the appropriate method for cleaning aluminum items?
    A. Using a stiff metal brush
    B. Using a water spray
    C. Using a circular motion
    D. Using a *to and fro* motion with the grain

25. Which of the following is TRUE regarding softened water?
    A. Increases the likelihood of mineral scale deposits
    B. Decreases the likelihood of mineral scale deposits
    C. Is not compatible with detergents
    D. Can cause rusting in metal instruments

KEY (CORRECT ANSWERS)

1.	C	11.	D
2.	A	12.	B
3.	C	13.	D
4.	A	14.	D
5.	C	15.	A
6.	B	16.	B
7.	C	17.	C
8.	B	18.	A
9.	A	19.	B
10.	C	20.	C

21. D
22. A
23. A
24. D
25. C

TEST 2

DIRECTIONS: Each question or incomplete statement is followed by several suggested answers or completions. Select the one that BEST answers the question or completes the statement. *PRINT THE LETTER OF THE CORRECT ANSWER IN THE SPACE AT THE RIGHT.*

1. Which of the following is FALSE regarding powered surgical instruments?   1.____
    A. Can be immersed
    B. Cannot be immersed
    C. Should be cleaned using a mechanical washer
    D. Should be cleaned at the point of use

2. What entity should provide the written cleaning instructions for surgical instruments?   2.____
    A. Manufacturer of the instrument
    B. The healthcare facility
    C. Manufacturer of the mechanical washer
    D. Manufacturer of the detergent

3. Which of the following is TRUE regarding pyrogens?   3.____
    A. They are fever producing substances.
    B. They are soil particles.
    C. They cause CD.
    D. They are microorganisms that remain after the sterilization process.

4. What is the appropriate pH level for detergents used for the majority of cleaning processes?   4.____
    A. High pH
    B. Low pH
    C. Neutral pH
    D. Varies according to water temperature and exposure time

5. When should instrument lubrication be performed?   5.____
    A. Immediately prior to use   B. Prior to cleaning
    C. After cleaning   D. After sterilization

6. What is the appropriate water temperature in order to avoid the coagulation of proteins?   6.____
    A. Below 24°C   B. Below 43°C   C. Above 43°C   D. Below 100°C

7. Which is the appropriate solution for cleaning instruments?   7.____
    A. Soap   B. Steam   C. Disinfectant   D. Detergent

8. Detergents used in mechanical cleaners should have which of the following characteristics?   8.____
    A. Low acidity   B. Low alkalinity
    C. Low foaming   D. Low temperature

9. Which of the following is classified as a high level disinfectant?
   A. Halogens and OPA
   B. Quaternary Ammonium Compounds and Phenolics
   C. Gluteraldehyde and OPA
   D. Gluteraldehyde and Phenolics

10. Which of the following is used during the thermal disinfection process?
    A. High pressure steam
    B. Heated water
    C. Heated gluteraldehyde
    D. Heated chemicals

11. Iodophors are a member of which disinfectant family?
    A. Halogens
    B. Alcohol
    C. Phenolics
    D. Quaternary Ammonium Compounds

12. Which process is used to completely destroy all forms of microorganisms?
    A. High-level disinfection
    B. Thermal disinfection
    C. Chemical disinfection
    D. Sterilization

13. For what time period must alcohol remain in wet contact with an item in order to achieve a reasonable level of disinfection?
    A. 3 minutes   B. 5 minutes   C. 10 minutes   D. 20 minutes

14. How are phenolics classified?
    A. Sterilants
    B. Intermediate to low-level disinfectants
    C. Intermediate to high-level disinfectants
    D. High-level disinfectants

15. Which chemicals are used on living tissue to slow the growth of micro-organisms?
    A. Antiseptics
    B. Disinfectants
    C. Gluteraldehydes
    D. Halogens

16. Which of the following are items that are introduced directly into the bloodstream or other normally sterile areas of the body?
    A. Immersible items
    B. Non-critical items
    C. Critical items
    D. Semi-critical items

17. What would be the BEST choice for high level disinfection of instruments?
    A. Iodophors   B. Phenolics   C. OPA   D. Chlorine

18. Thread-like tails attached to cells that permit bacteria to move through liquids are known as
    A. cytoplasm   B. tentacles   C. flagella   D. mitochondria

19. What type of stain test would be performed in order to identify bacterial traits?
    A. Ziehl-Neelsen
    B. Endospore
    C. Romanowsky
    D. Silver

20. Microorganisms that are capable of forming a thick wall around themselves that enables them to survive in adverse conditions are referred to as
    A. microbes
    B. spores
    C. viruses
    D. fungi

21. Cocci bacteria have what kind of shape?
    A. Cone
    B. Rod
    C. Spiral
    D. Spherical

22. Bacillus bacteria have what kind of shape?
    A. Cone
    B. Rod
    C. Spiral
    D. Spherical

23. Spirillum bacteria have what kind of shape?
    A. Cone
    B. Rod
    C. Spiral
    D. Spherical

24. What is the typical method for bacterial reproduction?
    A. Baeocyte Production
    B. Binary Fission
    C. Budding
    D. Intracellular offspring production

25. _____ bacteria are capable of growing in the absence of free oxygen.
    A. Aerobic
    B. Anaerobic
    C. Mesophilic
    D. Hydrophobic

KEY (CORRECT ANSWERS)

1.	B	11.	A
2.	A	12.	D
3.	A	13.	B
4.	C	14.	B
5.	C	15.	A
6.	B	16.	C
7.	D	17.	B
8.	C	18.	C
9.	C	19.	A
10.	B	20.	B

21. D
22. B
23. C
24. B
25. B

TEST 3

DIRECTIONS: Each question or incomplete statement is followed by several suggested answers or completions. Select the one that BEST answers the question or completes the statement. *PRINT THE LETTER OF THE CORRECT ANSWER IN THE SPACE AT THE RIGHT.*

1. What percentage of hospital in-patients will eventually develop a nosocomial (hospital-acquired) infection?
   A. 5%   B. 10%   C. 15%   D. 25%   1._____

2. The invasion of the human body tissue by microorganisms which multiply and produce a reaction is known as
   A. anaphylaxis   B. metastasis   C. infection   D. manifestation   2._____

3. What is the minimum length of time Central Service Technicians should scrub their hands during a routine hand washing?
   A. 15 seconds   B. 30 seconds   C. 45 seconds   D. 60 seconds   3._____

4. What is the recommended temperature for the decontamination area of Central Service?
   A. 40 - 45°F   B. 50 - 55°F   C. 60 – 65°F   D. 70 - 75°F   4._____

5. _____ is defined as an inanimate object that can transmit bacteria.
   A. Thermite   B. Dendrite   C. Fomite   D. Nitrite   5._____

6. The functional center of a cell that governs activity and heredity is known as
   A. nucleolus   B. flagella   C. cytoplasm   D. nucleus   6._____

7. The Ziehl-Neelsen stain is designed to classify bacteria according to which of the following?
   A. Appearance   B. Shape   C. Size   D. Color change   7._____

8. Using gram-stain classifications, Staphylococcus, Enterococcus, and Streptococcus are all examples of gram-_____ bacteria.
   A. negative   B. positive   C. neutral   D. apparent   8._____

9. _____ is defined as the state of being soiled or infected by contact with infectious organisms or other material.
   A. Contaminated   B. Infested   C. Delineated   D. Permeated   9._____

10. What is the size of the majority of bacteria?
    A. 1 – 2 microns   B. 3 – 4 microns
    C. 5 – 6 microns   D. 6 – 7 microns   10._____

11. Sunlight is lethal to pathogens in which stage?
    A. Reproductive   B. Active
    C. Transmission   D. Vegetative   11._____

12. The process of removing ions that have an electrical charge is referred to as
    A. reionizing B. deionizing C. neutralizing D. vaporizing

13. Which of the following refers to compounds that contain a positive electrical charge and exhibit germicidal properties?
    A. Anionic B. Cationic C. Ionizing D. Deionizing

14. A disinfectant is a chemical that kills the majority of pathogenic organisms EXCEPT
    A. fungi B. viruses C. bacteria D. spores

15. Which of the following refers to compounds that have a negative electrical charge and form a large group of synthetic detergents?
    A. Anionic B. Cationic C. Ionizing D. Deionizing

16. Which disinfectant is often used for environmental sanitation on objects such as floors, walls, and furniture and is incompatible with soaps?
    A. Gluteraldehyde
    B. Alcohol
    C. Ortho-Phthaldehyde
    D. Quaternary Ammonium Compounds

17. Which disinfectant is used for semi-critical devices such as endoscopes and has sterilant capabilities?
    A. Gluteraldehyde
    B. Alcohol
    C. Ortho-Phthaldehyde
    D. Quaternary Ammonium Compounds

18. Which disinfectant has been in use for many years, is often used to disinfect equipment, and is inactivated by organic soil?
    A. Gluteraldehyde
    B. Alcohol
    C. Ortho-Phthaldehyde
    D. Quaternary Ammonium Compounds

19. Which disinfectant is effective at room temperature, provides a fast and effective method for disinfecting a wide range of items, has high-level disinfection capabilities, but is not classified as a sterilant?
    A. Gluteraldehyde
    B. Alcohol
    C. Ortho-Phthaldehyde
    D. Quaternary Ammonium Compounds

20. The process of destruction of nearly all pathogenic microorganisms on an inanimate surface is referred to as
    A. disinfection B. sterilization
    C. washing D. decontamination

21. Which of the following is defined as the destruction of bacteria?
    A. Germicide
    B. Fungicide
    C. Bactericide
    D. Fomicide

22. Which of the following is defined as a small, proteinaceous, infectious disease causing agent that is believed to be the smallest infectious particle?
    A. Fungi
    B. Viruses
    C. Bacteria
    D. Prions

23. Which of the following is responsible for causing spongiform encephalopathy and Creutzfeltdt-Jakob disease?
    A. Fungi
    B. Viruses
    C. Bacteria
    D. Prions

24. Fingernail, tissues, and money are all examples of which of the following?
    A. Fomites
    B. Bacteria
    C. Fungi
    D. Viruses

25. During the final step in handwashing, the fingers should be rinsed with the fingertips in which direction?
    A. Up
    B. Down
    C. Parallel to the floor
    D. Intertwined

KEY (CORRECT ANSWERS)

1.	B	11.	D
2.	C	12.	B
3.	A	13.	B
4.	C	14.	D
5.	C	15.	A
6.	D	16.	D
7.	D	17.	A
8.	B	18.	B
9.	A	19.	C
10.	A	20.	A

21. C
22. D
23. D
24. A
25. A

TEST 4

DIRECTIONS: Each question or incomplete statement is followed by several suggested answers or completions. Select the one that BEST answers the question or completes the statement. *PRINT THE LETTER OF THE CORRECT ANSWER IN THE SPACE AT THE RIGHT.*

1. The most effective waterless hand antiseptics contain what concentration of alcohol?
   A. 30 – 50% B. 45 – 60% C. 50 – 75% D. 60 – 90%

   1._____

2. Which of the following is defined as the removal of contamination from an item to the extent necessary for further processing?
   A. Disinfection
   B. Cleaning
   C. Sterilization
   D. Decontamination

   2._____

3. How often should floors and work surfaces be cleaned?
   A. Hourly B. Daily C. Weekly D. Bi-weekly

   3._____

4. Which of the following statements is TRUE regarding the use of personal protective equipment in a decontamination area?
   A. The use of personal protective equipment is optional.
   B. Vinyl gloves is all that is required.
   C. Failure to wear personal protective equipment may result in disciplinary action.
   D. Gowns should be worn unless temperature is too warm.

   4._____

5. Which of the following should be obtained prior to cleaning and processing a medical device?
   A. Soap and water
   B. Alcohol and acetone
   C. Hospital policy on device processing
   D. Manufacturer's guidelines on device processing

   5._____

6. All of the following should be considerations when selecting a detergent EXCEPT
   A. quality of water
   B. amount of soil
   C. water temperature
   D. cost of detergent

   6._____

7. The clostridium botulinum bacteria is harbored in which of the following?
   A. Food B. Soil C. Air D. Water

   7._____

8. A solution with a pH level of 4 is considered to be
   A. neutral B. acidic C. alkaline D. contaminated

   8._____

9. A solution with a pH level of 12 is considered to be
   A. neutral B. acidic C. alkaline D. contaminated

   9._____

10. Which of the following are major non-living reservoirs for infectious diseases?
    A. Soil and gas
    B. Oil and water
    C. Gas and oil
    D. Soil and water

11. Why are alkaline detergents the BEST choice for mechanical washers?
    A. Increased friction during washing
    B. Decreased friction during washing
    C. Alkaline detergents should not be used by humans
    D. Acidic detergents promote corrosion within the mechanical washer

12. _____ detergent would be the proper detergent for removing severe stains on stainless steel instruments.
    A. Organic acid
    B. Organic alkaline
    C. Proteolytic enzyme
    D. Lipolytic enzyme

13. In order to prevent the formation of biofilm on instruments, the instruments should be rinsed with which of the following?
    A. Alcohol
    B. Saline
    C. Sterile water
    D. Distilled water

14. For what type of instrument would an ultrasonic lumen cleaner be used to clean?
    A. Laparoscopic instruments
    B. Endoscopic instruments
    C. Feeding tubes
    D. Sternal saws

15. Which is the proper process for mechanical washers to reduce the potential for instrument corrosion?
    A. Acid wash, alkaline rinse, regular rinse
    B. Alkaline wash, acid rinse, regular rinse
    C. Acid wash, acid rinse, regular rinse
    D. Alkaline wash, alkaline rinse, regular rinse

16. A biological indicator should contain how many spores?
    A. 10^1
    B. 10^4
    C. 10^6
    D. 10^8

17. Which of the following is a resistant, dormant structure that is formed inside of some bacteria and can withstand adverse conditions?
    A. Fomite
    B. Spore
    C. Endospore
    D. Exospore

18. Which piece of equipment loosens and removes debris through the use of sound waves traveling through liquid?
    A. Autoclave
    B. Ultrasonic cleaner
    C. Mechanical washer
    D. Hydrosonic cleaner

19. With what solution would you rinse instruments that have been processed in a liquid chemical sterilant?
    A. Alcohol
    B. Distilled water
    C. Sterile water
    D. Warm, soapy water

20. Which of the following is defined as the use of physical or chemical means to remove, inactivate, or destroy blood-borne pathogens from a surface or item?
    A. Cleaning
    B. Disinfection
    C. Sterilization
    D. Decontamination

21. The term _____ refers to microorganisms on contaminated items.
    A. bioburden
    B. biohazard
    C. biocleansing
    D. biotasking

22. What is the appropriate number of air exchanges in the decontamination area?
    A. 4
    B. 8
    C. 10
    D. 12

23. The ventilation system in the decontamination area must be maintained at _____ pressure.
    A. negative
    B. positive
    C. neutral
    D. zero

24. What is the appropriate pH level for a neutral solution?
    A. 5
    B. 7
    C. 9
    D. 11

25. Which solution should NEVER be used to remove gross soil from instruments?
    A. Alcohol
    B. Sterile water
    C. Distilled water
    D. Saline Solution

KEY (CORRECT ANSWERS)

1.	D	11.	B
2.	B	12.	A
3.	B	13.	D
4.	C	14.	A
5.	D	15.	B
6.	D	16.	C
7.	B	17.	C
8.	B	18.	B
9.	C	19.	C
10.	D	20.	D

21.	A
22.	C
23.	A
24.	B
25.	D

EXAMINATION SECTION

TEST 1

DIRECTIONS: Each question or incomplete statement is followed by several suggested answers or completions. Select the one that BEST answers the question or completes the statement. *PRINT THE LETTER OF THE CORRECT ANSWER IN THE SPACE AT THE RIGHT.*

1. All of the following are packaging systems used to maintain, store, and transport sterile surgical equipment EXCEPT
   A. peel pouching
   B. woven material wrappers
   C. porous containers
   D. rigid containers

   1.____

2. Which statement is NOT one of the four primary objectives for all packaging materials?
   A. They must allow penetration of the chosen sterilant and be compatible with any other requirements of the sterilization process.
   B. They must be able to maintain the sterility of package contents after opening.
   C. They must create a package that can be opened without contaminating the contents by the user.
   D. They must permit the contents to be sterile at point of use.

   2.____

3. The packaging system should be tamper-_____ so a package opened in error cannot be resealed without complete reprocessing.
   A. resistant   B. consistent   C. evident   D. dependent

   3.____

4. For what reason can Tyvek peel pouches not be used with steam sterilization?
   A. Instruments will not be completely sterilized.
   B. It will contaminate other instruments in the load.
   C. It will melt.
   D. It will disintegrate.

   4.____

5. The proper size for a single or double peel package should have how much clearance on all sides of the package?
   A. ⅛ inch   B. ¼ inch   C. ⅗ inch   D. ½ inch

   5.____

6. Curved instruments should be placed with the curved end toward the _____ of the pouch to avoid punctures.
   A. plastic side
   B. paper side
   C. open end
   D. closed end

   6.____

15

7. Instruments should be placed with the handles toward the _____ to allow the scrub person at the sterile field to easily remove the instruments when opening the pouch.
   A. plastic side
   B. paper side
   C. closed end
   D. pre-sealed end

8. What should be placed inside the pouch next to the surgical instrument so the color change can be seen through the plastic side of the pouch?
   A. Biological indicator
   B. Toxicological indicator
   C. Chemical indicator
   D. Environmental indicator

9. When using self-sealed pouches, the fold lines provided by the manufacturer should be _____ to prevent small openings between the package and the sealant.
   A. overlapped
   B. underlapped
   C. disregarded
   D. strictly followed

10. When manually sealing a pouch, there should be ample space at the end of the pouch for users to use their _____ to open the package and present the contents aseptically into the sterile field.
    A. hand
    B. first finger
    C. thumb
    D. middle finger

11. Operating room personnel typically prefer _____ pouched of multiple instruments because the inner pouch keeps the instruments together when opened onto a sterile field.
    A. single
    B. double
    C. Tyvek
    D. woven

12. All of the following information should be recorded on the plastic side of a pouch package EXCEPT
    A. item name
    B. storage location
    C. date wrapped
    D. name of package assembler

13. Writing on the paper side of the pouch can compromise
    A. legibility
    B. usability
    C. sterility
    D. availability

14. Plastic paper pouches should not be used within wrapped sets or rigid containers because the pouches may be positioned in a way that interferes with all of the following EXCEPT
    A. air removal
    B. heat penetration
    C. sterilant contact
    D. drying

15. Woven wrapping materials are usually NOT produced with which material?
    A. 100% cotton
    B. Cotton-silk
    C. Cotton-Polyester
    D. Synthetic blends

16. Which of the following is NOT required for woven materials before each use?
    A. Laundering   B. De-linting
    C. Inspection for holes D. Sorted according to size

17. When using woven materials, instruments must be wrapped in a way that facilitates _____ presentation of the contents.
    A. ready-to-use   B. septic   C. aseptic   D. flawless

18. With how many layers should an instrument tray be wrapped?
    A. 1   B. 2   C. 3   D. 4

19. Wrapped packages to be sterilized by steam may require a _____ to be placed underneath the item to prevent package rips and tears during storage and eliminate moisture that occurs during the steam cycle.
    A. wire rack   B. Styrofoam tray
    C. absorbent towel   D. sterile drape

20. Non-absorbent materials must be used under items when disposable wraps are used for instruments to be processed with _____ sterilization.
    A. ozone
    B. steam
    C. dry heat
    D. hydrogen peroxide gas plasma vapor

21. What occurs as hydrogen peroxide gas gets absorbed?
    A. Corroding the instruments.
    B. Producing biofilm on the instruments
    C. Depleting the sterilant in the chamber
    D. Increasing the temperature in the chamber

22. What occurs if the sterilant gets depleted in the chamber?
    A. The sterilization cycle gets cancelled.
    B. The sterilization cycle is extended.
    C. The sterilization cycle is shortened.
    D. All instruments will need reprocessing.

23. The ability of sterilization wrappers to maintain the content's sterility has been historically based on how many layers of wrap material?
    A. 1   B. 2   C. 3   D. 4

24. What type of wrappers are available that are sealed together on two sides and allow the use of a simultaneous envelope fold wrapping technique?
    A. Tyvek   B. Polypropylene
    C. Kraft paper   D. Polyethylene

25. What is used to secure the last fold of the inside wrap? 25._____
    A. Tape
    B. Paper clips
    C. Rubber bands
    D. Second layer of wrap

KEY (CORRECT ANSWERS)

1.	C		11.	B
2.	B		12.	A
3.	C		13.	C
4.	C		14.	B
5.	B		15.	B
6.	A		16.	D
7.	D		17.	C
8.	C		18.	B
9.	D		19.	C
10.	C		20.	D

21.	D
22.	A
23.	B
24.	B
25.	D

TEST 2

DIRECTIONS: Each question or incomplete statement is followed by several suggested answers or completions. Select the one that BEST answers the question or completes the statement. *PRINT THE LETTER OF THE CORRECT ANSWER IN THE SPACE AT THE RIGHT.*

1. Wrap materials should always be used according to
   A. hospital policy
   B. managerial direction
   C. manufacturer guidelines
   D. OSHA requirements

   1.____

2. Writing directly on the wrapping material will compromise _____ of the instruments.
   A. integrity
   B. sterility
   C. usability
   D. reusability

   2.____

3. The weight of the tray or other item should not exceed how much, including the container and instruments?
   A. 10 lbs.
   B. 15 lbs.
   C. 20 lbs.
   D. 25 lbs.

   3.____

4. What can happen if a wrapped package is handled before it is thoroughly cooled?
   A. External wrapping may disintegrate.
   B. Instruments may become corroded.
   C. Bacteria can be pulled from human hands.
   D. Moisture can be introduced to the package.

   4.____

5. Which of the following is NOT a factor for selecting a rigid container?
   A. Cost of the instruments
   B. Size of instrument set
   C. Ease of assembly
   D. Ease of cleaning

   5.____

6. Which of the following is NOT an item used to maintain rigid containers?
   A. Locks
   B. Filters
   C. Labels
   D. Gauges

   6.____

7. Most rigid containers require an integrity lock on _____ of the cart.
   A. top
   B. bottom
   C. right side
   D. both sides

   7.____

8. What is concerning about the use of rigid containers? Lack of _____ indicator.
   A. biological
   B. chemical
   C. environmental
   D. toxicological

   8.____

9. What is the purpose of an integrity lock on the rigid container?
   A. Indicates how long the container has been in storage
   B. Reveals dates when preventative maintenance is required
   C. Indicates container has not been tampered with
   D. Allows containers to be stacked on top of each other

   9.____

10. What is NOT a concern when selecting the packaging system to be used?
    A. Sterilization method
    B. Approval by the Environmental Protection Agency
    C. Size of contents
    D. Weight of contents

11. What is the one purpose of the paper side of a peel pouch?
    A. To allow sterilant to enter the pouch
    B. To allow direct visualization of the contents
    C. To provide added protection to the contents
    D. To permit sterile handling of the pouch

12. Which statement is TRUE about the use of peel pouches when processing instruments with sharp tips?
    A. Longer processing time is required.
    B. Higher processing temperature is required.
    C. Paper pouches should never be used.
    D. Clear-vented tip protectors should be used.

13. Which of the following should occur prior to sealing a peel pouch?
    A. Excess air should be removed.
    B. Identification information should be written on the pouch.
    C. Hydrogen peroxide gas plasma should be introduced into the pouch.
    D. Ethylene oxide should be introduced into the pouch.

14. Which of the following is NOT a purpose for filter and locking mechanisms of rigid containers?
    A. Allow for removal of moisture
    B. Promote drying
    C. Allow for aseptic presentation
    D. Provide easier method of transport

15. Peel pouches should be labeled with which of the following?
    A. Wax marker   B. Pencil
    C. Ballpoint pen   D. Permanent marker

16. If a non-perforated tray is used for the sterilization of instruments, how must it be placed on the sterilizer rack?
    A. Flat   B. Tilted   C. Sideways   D. Upside-down

17. How should basin sets be prepared for sterilization?
    A. Basins stacked on top of one another
    B. Non-absorbent material between each basin
    C. Absorbent material between each basin
    D. Basins should be prepared individually

18. Which of the following is NOT a critical parameter for heat sealing paper-plastic pouches?
    A. Temperature   B. Pressure   C. Dwell time   D. Humidity

3 (#2)

19. Sterilant penetration can be inhibited by which of the following?   19.____
    A. Using a wrapper that is too small
    B. Using a wrapper that is too large
    C. Failing to wrap an instrument
    D. Using paper wrapping

20. When rigid containers are processed in a steam sterilizer, they must be   20.____
    placed on the cart in which position?
    A. Flat   B. Tilted   C. Sideways   D. Upside-down

21. With respect to rigid sterilization container testing, which term defines   21.____
    the sterilizer's ability to sterilize under actual use conditions?
    A. Adequate load testing   B. Minimum load testing
    C. Maximum load testing   D. Moderate load testing

22. Which of the following is TRUE of a capsule?   22.____
    A. It is less difficult to kill than vegetative bacteria.
    B. It is more difficult to kill than a spore.
    C. It is resistant to heat and chemicals.
    D. It is easily killed by antibiotics.

23. OSHA requires that containers of potentially infectious materials be   23.____
    which of the following?
    A. Leak-proof   B. Spill-proof
    C. Water-proof   D. Shatter-proof

24. Rigid containers are considered to be a medical device and must have a   24.____
    510(k) clearance from which agency?
    A. Occupational Safety and Health Administration
    B. Food and Drug Administration
    C. National Institute of Health
    D. Centers for Disease Control and Prevention

25. If a wrapper will be used as the sterile field, how far over the edge of the   25.____
    table must the wrapper extend?
    A. 2 inches   B. 4 inches   C. 6 inches   D. 8 inches

KEY (CORRECT ANSWERS)

1.	C	11.	A
2.	B	12.	D
3.	D	13.	A
4.	C	14.	D
5.	A	15.	D
6.	D	16.	B
7.	D	17.	C
8.	B	18.	D
9.	C	19.	B
10.	B	20.	A

21. C
22. C
23. A
24. B
25. C

TEST 3

DIRECTIONS: Each question or incomplete statement is followed by several suggested answers or completions. Select the one that BEST answers the question or completes the statement. *PRINT THE LETTER OF THE CORRECT ANSWER IN THE SPACE AT THE RIGHT.*

1. Where should the chemical indicator be placed when sterilizing two large basins with smaller basins in one set?
    A. In the large basins
    B. In the small basins
    C. In the top and bottom basins
    D. One indicator in a large basin and one indicator in a small basin

    1.____

2. What is the proper method for placing ring-handled instruments in an instrument tray?
    A. Arrange the instruments in the order in which they will be used
    B. Lock the handles to prevent damage during sterilization
    C. Unlock the handles and open the instruments
    D. Arrange the instrument in order by size

    2.____

3. Which of the following is NOT a purpose of wicking materials?
    A. Cushion instruments from force of steam sterilizer chambers
    B. Permit air removal
    C. Promote steam penetration
    D. Facilitate drying

    3.____

4. Which of the following is NOT an acceptable sterilization packaging material?
    A. Twills
    B. Barrier cloth
    C. Muslin
    D. Canvas

    4.____

5. The Food and Drug Administration classifies sterilization packaging as a Class _____ Medical Device.
    A. II   B. III   C. IV   D. V

    5.____

6. Which of the following is FALSE regarding the regulatory requirements of sterile packaging?
    A. 510(k) is required
    B. Regulated by AAMI
    C. Class II Medical Device
    D. Regulated by FDA

    6.____

7. Which statement is TRUE regarding disposable non-woven wraps?
    A. Ineffective bacterial barrier
    B. Marginal bacterial barrier
    C. Effective bacterial barrier
    D. Reduces costs for disposal

    7.____

8. Which of the following is FALSE regarding containers?
   A. Most durable sterilization packaging
   B. Provides optimum barrier to protect contents
   C. Easy to use and most versatile
   D. Compatible with all sterilization methods

9. Cleaning anodized aluminum containers requires the use of what type of detergent?
   A. Acidic pH
   B. Neutral pH
   C. Alkaline pH
   D. Highly alkaline pH

10. Event related shelf life is based on which of the following principles?
    A. Time is the determining factor for sterile products becoming contaminated.
    B. Specific events are responsible for sterile products becoming contaminated.
    C. The integrity of the package is not a determining factor in establishing the sterility of the contents.
    D. The method of sterilization is not a determining factor in establishing the sterility of the contents.

11. Which of the following are nationally recognized resources that contain essential information for the selection and evaluation of packaging systems?
    A. AAMI and AORN Standards and Recommended Practices
    B. JCAHO Standards
    C. EPA Regulations
    D. FDA Regulations

12. Sterilization packaging systems have an impact on all of the following EXCEPT
    A. surgical instruments
    B. nosocomial infections
    C. healthcare costs
    D. competency of surgical staff

13. For wrapped packages, where should the information be documented?
    A. Not required for wrapped packages
    B. On the instruments themselves
    C. On the wrap
    D. On the sterilization indicator tape

14. Which statement is FALSE regarding elastomer bands?
    A. They are acceptable for inside closures.
    B. They are acceptable for outside closures.
    C. Proper size must be chosen.
    D. They should be used only if the manufacturer explicitly recommends their use.

15. Which statement is FALSE regarding tip protectors? 15.____
    A. They should be steam permeable.
    B. They should fit loosely.
    C. They should fit tightly.
    D. They should be used according to manufacturer's guidelines.

16. _____ wrapping is defined as items being wrapped twice, thus creating a 16.____
    pouch within a pouch.
    A. Simultaneous   B. Sequential   C. Aseptic   D. Antiseptic

17. _____ wrapping is defined as the package being wrapped once with a 17.____
    special double-layered synthetic non-woven material bound on the sides.
    A. Simultaneous   B. Sequential   C. Aseptic   D. Antiseptic

18. A(n) _____ fold is most commonly used for smaller items. 18.____
    A. envelope   B. square   C. rigid   D. parallel

19. A(n) _____ fold is most commonly used on larger packs. 19.____
    A. envelope   B. square   C. rigid   D. parallel

20. On what surface should a textile wrap be inspected for holes? 20.____
    A. Sterile table   B. Sterile countertop
    C. Lighted table   D. Any stainless steel surface

21. If holes are appreciated in woven materials, through what method should 21.____
    they be mended?
    A. Stitched   B. Vulcanized patches
    C. Taped   D. Glued

22. Fabrics that have been previously sterilized can be dehydrated and lead 22.____
    to _____ if not pre-conditioned properly.
    A. underheating   B. superheating
    C. supercooling   D. excessive moisture absorbance

23. The manufacturer should provide all of the following for rigid containers 23.____
    EXCEPT
    A. information on type of filters or wraps
    B. locations of the most challenging areas for placement of biological
       indicators and internal chemical indicators for routing monitoring and
       product testing
    C. procedures for inspection and routine maintenance of the containment
       devices
    D. MSDS sheets for all acceptable cleaners and disinfectants

24. Prior to assembly of a rigid container, the gaskets should be inspected to 24.____
    ensure all of the following EXCEPT
    A. pliability   B. securely fastened
    C. without breaks   D. bioburden

25. To facilitate the removal of moisture, basin sets should be prepared so that all basins are oriented to face
    A. upward
    B. downward
    C. the same direction
    D. opposite directions

KEY (CORRECT ANSWERS)

1.	C		11.	A
2.	C		12.	D
3.	A		13.	D
4.	D		14.	A
5.	A		15.	C
6.	B		16.	B
7.	C		17.	A
8.	D		18.	A
9.	B		19.	B
10.	B		20.	C

21. B
22. B
23. D
24. D
25. C

TEST 4

DIRECTIONS: Each question or incomplete statement is followed by several suggested answers or completions. Select the one that BEST answers the question or completes the statement. *PRINT THE LETTER OF THE CORRECT ANSWER IN THE SPACE AT THE RIGHT.*

1. Devices with lumens such as catheters, needles, suctions, and tubing should be flushed with what substance just prior to packaging? 1.____
   A. Alcohol
   B. Hydrogen peroxide
   C. Distilled water
   D. Acetone

2. It is NOT appropriate to put paper/plastic pouches within which of the following? 2.____
   A. Wrapped sets
   B. Appropriate foam products
   C. Paper autoclave bags
   D. Perforated mesh-bottom baskets with lids

3. Which of the following statements is TRUE regarding metal items? 3.____
   A. They should never be placed in the sterilizer.
   B. They should be placed over textile packages.
   C. They should never be placed over textile packages.
   D. They should be sterilized separately.

4. Which of the following is defined as the process of sterilizing a packaged item? 4.____
   A. Flash sterilization
   B. Terminal Sterilization
   C. Point of use processing
   D. Shock sterilization

5. Which of the following is the process by which unwrapped instruments are steam sterilized for immediate use? 5.____
   A. Flash sterilization
   B. Terminal sterilization
   C. Point of use processing
   D. Shock sterilization

6. Which agency does NOT have established guidelines, standards, and recommendations for flash sterilization? 6.____
   A. AORN   B. AAMI   C. EPA   D. JCAHO

7. For what reason was flash sterilization originally intended? 7.____
   A. Save time
   B. Save money
   C. Increase volume
   D. Emergencies

8. Which type of cycle CANNOT accomplish flash sterilization? 8.____
   A. Pre-vacuum
   B. Post-vacuum
   C. Express
   D. Gravity displacement

9. What type of packaging materials are NOT suitable for ozone sterilization?
   A. Non-woven materials
   B. Woven materials
   C. Polyethylene pouches
   D. Anodized aluminum containers using non-cellulose disposable filters

10. Which of the following would NOT be a factor leading to superheating and sterilization failure?
    A. Relaundering
    B. Over-drying
    C. Heat pressing
    D. Storage in areas of low humidity

11. Sterilized count sheets should never be placed in which of the following?
    A. Paper/paper pouches
    B. Paper/plastic pouches
    C. Rigid containers
    D. Plastic/plastic pouches

12. Pre-purchase biological testing of rigid containers should be performed under the standards of which agency?
    A. Food and Drug Administration
    B. Association for the Advancement of Medical Instrumentation
    C. Occupational Safety and Health Administration
    D. Centers for Disease Control and Prevention

13. How many chemical indicators/integrators should be placed inside rigid containers?
    A. 1   B. 2   C. 3   D. 4

14. Where should chemical indicators/integrators be placed inside of rigid containers?
    A. Top and bottom
    B. One on left side and one on the right side
    C. One in each of two opposite corners of the inside basket
    D. Side by side in the middle of the inside basket

15. Where should a chemical indicator/integrator be placed in multi-level wrapped sets?
    A. One on each level
    B. Top and bottom of each level
    C. One in two opposite corners of every level
    D. Side by side in the middle of every level

16. Placing instruments inside the steam sterilizer 10-15 minutes with the door closed prior to starting the cycle to avoid wet pack issues is known as
    A. preloading
    B. preconditioning
    C. pre-wrapping
    D. pre-sterilizing

17. An instrument tray that contains instruments and supplies for an entire procedure is known as a(n) _____ tray.
    A. surgical   B. floor   C. exam   D. single use

18. During processing, the barrel and the glass syringe should be separated by which of the following?
    A. Kraft paper
    B. Sterile drape
    C. Wicking material
    D. 4 x 4 non-sterile radiopaque gauze

19. If a bottle of distilled water is used to flush a device with a lumen, how long before the open bottle of distilled water should be disposed?
    A. 6 hours   B. 8 hours   C. 12 hours   D. 24 hours

20. Residues left on eye instruments can cause which of the following?
    A. Toxic Anterior Segment Syndrome
    B. Creutzfeldt-Jakob Syndrome
    C. Transmissible spongiform encephalopathy
    D. Nosocomial infections

21. The American Society of Cataract and Refractive Surgery has recommended the use of which of the following products for the rinsing of eye instruments prior to sterilization?
    A. Sterile deionized water   B. Alcohol
    C. Betadine   D. Hydrogen peroxide

22. Which agency has advised that laryngoscope blades should be packaged in some way and will check to ensure that blades are stored in a way that will prevent recontamination?
    A. Joint Commission
    B. Food and Drug Administration
    C. State Department of Health
    D. Environmental Protection Agency

23. Laryngoscope handles should only be placed in peel packs for what reason?
    A. Convenience   B. Storage   C. Patient use   D. Sterilization

24. Instruments with removable parts must be _____ prior to using before being placed in trays unless the manufacturer's instructions specify otherwise.
    A. left intact   B. decontaminated
    C. disassembled   D. sterilized

25. Trays containing more than one complex instrument should be _____ tested to ensure that proper sterilization conditions occur inside the tray.
    A. biologically   B. chemically
    C. toxicology   D. cytogenically

KEY (CORRECT ANSWERS)

1.	C	11.	C
2.	A	12.	B
3.	C	13.	B
4.	B	14.	C
5.	A	15.	A
6.	C	16.	B
7.	D	17.	B
8.	B	18.	D
9.	B	19.	D
10.	A	20.	A

21.	A
22.	A
23.	B
24.	C
25.	A

EXAMINATION SECTION

TEST 1

DIRECTIONS: Each question or incomplete statement is followed by several suggested answers or completions. Select the one that BEST answers the question or completes the statement. *PRINT THE LETTER OF THE CORRECT ANSWER IN THE SPACE AT THE RIGHT.*

1. What is the MOST efficient type of dry heat sterilizer?　　　　　　　　　　1.____
   A. Mechanical convection sterilizer　　B. Gravity convection sterilizer
   C. Dynamic air removal sterilizer　　　D. Special purpose dry heat oven

2. What does the term *superheated steam* refer to?　　　　　　　　　　　　2.____
   A. Moist steam at sea level
   B. Type of steam necessary for high temperature sterilization
   C. Dry steam
   D. Steam that has chemicals added in order to increase temperature

3. What would be the recommended exposure time for a dry heat sterilization　　3.____
   load that was run at an exposure temperature of 320°F (160°C)?
   A. 1 hour　　　B. 1.5 hours　　　C. 2 hours　　　D. 2.5 hours

4. Where should items with solid bottoms be located when loading a steam　　4.____
   sterilizer?
   A. On the edge　　　　　　　　　B. Loaded first
   C. Placed in an upright position　　D. In a wire basket

5. _____ tests use live bacterial spores to challenge the efficacy of the　　　5.____
   sterilization process and provide a direct measure of lethality.
   A. Chemical indicator　　　B. Biological
   C. Chemical integrator　　　D. Ampulization

6. What must be done in order to elevate the temperature of a steam sterilizer?　6.____
   A. Inject boiler amines　　　　B. Achieve ambient pressure
   C. Decrease steam pressure　　D. Increase steam pressure

7. What is the consequence of having an object with a high bioburden?　　　7.____
   A. More difficult to sterilize
   B. Will take less time to sterilize
   C. Need to load more biological tests
   D. Will take longer to cool after sterilization

8. Which statement is TRUE regarding paper/plastic sterilization pouches?　　8.____
   A. Should only be used for dry heat sterilization processes
   B. Should not be placed inside wrapped sets or containers
   C. Are not suitable for steam sterilization processes
   D. Are used to package wood and cork products for sterilization

9. How frequently should the strainer of a sterilizer be removed and cleaned?
   A. When the machine gauge indicates cleaning is necessary
   B. Daily
   C. Weekly
   D. Monthly

10. What bacterial spore is used for testing steam sterilizers?
    A. Geobacillus stearothermophilus   B. Bacillus atrophaeus
    C. Pseudomonas aeruginosa   D. Bacillus subtillus

11. What sterilization quality assurance measurements are designed to provided a written record of sterilizer cycle activity?
    A. Bowie Dick tests
    B. Mechanical recording charts/printouts
    C. Biological tests
    D. Chemical integrators

12. What statement is TRUE regarding chemical indicators?
    A. They provide a visual indication that an item was exposed to a sterilization process
    B. They prove that an item is sterile
    C. They provide information about bacterial spore kill within the sterilizer
    D. They prove that the sterilizer did not damage heat sensitive items

13. Which of the following refers to the amount of time required to kill 90% of the microorganisms present on an object?
    A. Exposure time   B. D-value
    C. Time-weighted average   D. Sterilization cycle

14. What do instrument washer sterilizers provide?
    A. Dry heat sterilization
    B. Terminal sterilization
    C. Flash sterilization for immediate patient use
    D. A decontamination process

15. Which of the following is TRUE when a sterilizer has successfully killed all the bacterial spores in a biological test?
    A. It is called a positive test.
    B. It is called a negative test.
    C. An alarm will sound at the completion of the cycle.
    D. It is taken out of service until it is repaired.

16. Where should Bowie-Dick tests be performed?
    A. Washer/sterilizers
    B. Downward displacement sterilizers
    C. Ethylene oxide sterilizers
    D. Dynamic air removal steam sterilizers

17. Where would information about load specific load contents be obtained in the event of a load recall?
    A. The procedure manual
    B. The sterilization log
    C. The Central Service Supervisor
    D. The Hospital Safety Director

18. How often should sterilizer recording charts and/or printouts be checked?
    A. Hourly
    B. During and at the end of each cycle
    C. Every shift
    D. Every 24 hours

19. What are the two most common temperatures used in steam sterilization?
    A. 320° and 350° - 355°F
    B. 250° and 270° - 275°F
    C. 120° and 140°F
    D. 100° and 130°F

20. Impregnated gauze strips may be sterilized through the use of _____ sterilization.
    A. dry heat
    B. ethylene oxide
    C. steam
    D. hydrogen peroxide gas plasma

21. Which of the following is an absorbent material that allows for air removal, steam penetration, and facilitates air drying?
    A. Sterile gauze
    B. Wicking material
    C. Surgical drapes
    D. Paper towels

22. What is the point of use process by which unwrapped instruments are sterilized for immediate use when an emergency situation arises?
    A. High temperature sterilization
    B. Low temperature sterilization
    C. Flash sterilization
    D. Steam sterilization

23. Which of the following is a liquid oxidizing agent that is an effective biocide at low temperatures and is used in a sterilization system that processes immersible instruments for immediate use?
    A. Peracetic acid
    B. Hydrogen peroxide
    C. Ethylene oxide
    D. Sulfuric acid

24. What is the MOST commonly used method of sterilization used in healthcare facilities?
    A. Flash sterilization
    B. Steam sterilization
    C. Ethylene oxide sterilization
    D. Hydrogen peroxide gas plasma sterilization

25. What type of steam sterilizer is used for sterilizing liquids?
    A. Mechanical convection sterilizer
    B. Gravity air displacement sterilizer
    C. Dynamic air removal sterilizer
    D. Special purpose dry heat oven

KEY (CORRECT ANSWERS)

1.	A		11.	B
2.	C		12.	A
3.	C		13.	B
4.	A		14.	D
5.	B		15.	B
6.	D		16.	D
7.	A		17.	B
8.	B		18.	B
9.	B		19.	B
10.	A		20.	A

21. B
22. C
23. A
24. B
25. B

TEST 2

DIRECTIONS: Each question or incomplete statement is followed by several suggested answers or completions. Select the one that BEST answers the question or completes the statement. *PRINT THE LETTER OF THE CORRECT ANSWER IN THE SPACE AT THE RIGHT.*

1. _____ sterilization is the process of sterilizing an item that is packaged?
    A. Steam
    B. Flash
    C. Terminal
    D. Low temperature

    1._____

2. Which of the following is a prion disease that demands that instruments be processed differently than standard protocols?
    A. Hepatitis C
    B. Creutzfeldt-Jakob Disease
    C. HIV
    D. Crohn's Disease

    2._____

3. The process by which a device is actively subjected to moving air to facilitate the removal of ethylene oxide gas is known as
    A. ventilation   B. oxidation   C. aeration   D. detoxification

    3._____

4. Which of the following is a compound in which chlorine is combined with another element or radical such as a salt or hydrochloric acid?
    A. Chloride   B. Chlorite   C. Chlorate   D. Chlorine

    4._____

5. What is defined as the measurement of the ability of water to carry an electrical current?
    A. Electricity   B. Conductivity   C. Excitability   D. Permeability

    5._____

6. Which of the following is defined as the diffusion of water through a semi-permeable membrane to eliminate impurities in the water?
    A. Osmosis
    B. Reverse osmosis
    C. Hydrosis
    D. Meiosis

    6._____

7. A liquid solution having the sediment or solids stirred up to appear as a cloudy silicate from a mineral derived from a silica such as quartz, sand or opal is defined as
    A. liquidity   B. turbidity   C. solubility   D. separability

    7._____

8. Which is defined as the unit of measure that measures the amount of resistance to an electrical current?
    A. Volts   B. Joules   C. Watts   D. Ohms

    8._____

9. Which of the following is a solution to remove white, hard-to-remove, substances that sometimes appears on sinks and equipment?
    A. Deionizers   B. Desiccants   C. Descales   D. Decontaminants

    9._____

10. _____ tests are used to evaluate the efficacy of an air removal system of a steam sterilizer.
    A. Biological   B. Chemical   C. Bowie-Dick   D. Leak

    10._____

11. A(n) _____ trap is the portion of a steam sterilizer that measures steam temperature and automatically controls the flow of air and condensate from the sterilizer chamber.
    A. thermostatic   B. chemostatic   C. biostatic   D. electrostatic

12. Steam sterilization heats items within the load using a heat transfer process called
    A. conduction   B. ventilation   C. convection   D. dilution

13. Dry heat sterilization heats items within the load using a heat transfer process called
    A. conduction   B. ventilation   C. convection   D. dilution

14. Which of the following is the NEWEST low temperature sterilization process?
    A. Ethylene oxide gas
    B. Hydrogen peroxide
    C. Peracetic acid
    D. Ozone

15. Which method of low temperature sterilization has been in use since the 1960s?
    A. Ethylene oxide gas
    B. Hydrogen peroxide
    C. Peracetic acid
    D. Ozone

16. What is the proper cycle time for items sterilized using hydrogen peroxide gas plasma?
    A. Less than 1 hour
    B. 1 hour
    C. 2 hours
    D. 4 hours

17. What is the proper cycle time for items using ozone sterilization?
    A. 2 hours   B. 4 hours   C. 6 hours   D. 8 hours

18. What is the proper 140°F aeration time for items sterilized with ethylene oxide?
    A. 2 hours   B. 4 hours   C. 6 hours   D. 8 hours

19. What is the bacterial spore used to test ethylene oxide sterilization cycles?
    A. Geobacillus stearothermophilus
    B. Bacillus atrophaeus
    C. Pseudomonas aeruginosa
    D. Bacillus subtillus

20. What is the appropriate cycle time for items sterilized using ethylene oxide sterilization?
    A. 6 hours   B. 8 hours   C. 10 hours   D. 12+ hours

21. Which agency has exposure standards for chemical sterilants?
    A. Food and Drug Administration
    B. Occupational Health and Safety Administration
    C. Centers for Disease Control and Prevention
    D. National Institute of Health

3 (#2)

22. Which agency requires that sterilants be rigorously tested prior to being marketed?
    A. Food and Drug Administration
    B. Occupational Health and Safety Administration
    C. Centers for Disease Control and Prevention
    D. National Institute of Health

22.____

23. Large instruments in a set should be evenly distributed to prevent the formation of which of the following?
    A. Condensation   B. Silicates   C. Bacteria   D. Prions

23.____

24. Which agency is responsible for regulating environmental disinfectants?
    A. Food and Drug Administration
    B. Occupational Health and Safety Administration
    C. Centers for Disease Control and Prevention
    D. Environmental Protection Agency

24.____

25. Medical-grade Kraft paper CANNOT be used with which of the following sterilization processes?
    A. Low temperature   B. Low temperature gas plasma
    C. Ethylene oxide   D. Ozone

25.____

KEY (CORRECT ANSWERS)

1.	C		11.	A
2.	B		12.	C
3.	C		13.	A
4.	A		14.	D
5.	B		15.	A
6.	B		16.	A
7.	B		17.	B
8.	D		18.	D
9.	C		19.	B
10.	C		20.	D

21.	B
22.	A
23.	A
24.	D
25.	B

TEST 3

DIRECTIONS: Each question or incomplete statement is followed by several suggested answers or completions. Select the one that BEST answers the question or completes the statement. *PRINT THE LETTER OF THE CORRECT ANSWER IN THE SPACE AT THE RIGHT.*

1. How are items that have a large dollar value but are used infrequently classified during cycle counts?
   A. Class A   B. Class B   C. Class C   D. Class D
   1._____

2. For non-tabletop steam sterilizes, where is the steam generated?
   A. Condenser   B. Generator   C. Boiler   D. Refractor
   2._____

3. What type of indicator is autoclave tape considered?
   A. Class 1   B. Class 2   C. Class 4   D. Class 5
   3._____

4. Which part of the steam sterilizer produces heat inside the chamber to prevent condensation from forming on the chamber walls?
   A. Boiler   B. Jacket   C. Generator   D. Condenser
   4._____

5. What process can minimize the need for frequent instrument reprocessing?
   A. Proper stock rotation
   B. Proper handling of materials
   C. Proper use by operating room staff
   D. Proper method of sterilization
   5._____

6. What is the coldest part of the sterilizer?
   A. Boiler   B. Jacket   C. Drain line   D. Condenser
   6._____

7. Gradual heating of packs occurs during which phase of the steam sterilization cycle?
   A. Pre-heating   B. Cooling   C. Conditioning   D. Drying
   7._____

8. What is the MOST important thing to remember when double-peel pouching?
   A. The outer pouch must completely encompass the inner pouch.
   B. The inner pouch must lay flat inside the outer pouch.
   C. The outer pouch must be twice as large as the inner pouch.
   D. The inner pouch must not touch the outer pouch.
   8._____

9. Which of the following BEST describes a minimum exposure time, temperature, and pressure for pre-vacuum steam sterilization of wrapped items?
   A. 4 minutes at 270°F and 28-30 pounds per square inch
   B. 3 minutes at 270°F and 38-40 pounds per square inch
   C. 15 minutes at 250°F and 28-30 pounds per square inch
   D. 30 minutes at 250°F and 28-40 pounds per square inch
   9._____

10. Incoming saturated steam should be within what range of dryness?
    A. 5% - 6%   B. 10% - 12%   C. 51% - 55%   D. 97% - 100%
    10._____

11. What will result if there is a failure to remove all air from a package within a steam sterilizer?
    A. Excess steam penetration
    B. Poor steam penetration
    C. Corrosion of instruments
    D. Decreased bioburden

12. Steam is exhausted from the sterilizer through which of the following?
    A. Boiler
    B. Generator
    C. Jacket
    D. Chamber drain line

13. For what reason must textile packs be placed on their sides for sterilization?
    A. To ensure they fit properly in the sterilizer
    B. To avoid corrosion of instruments
    C. To facilitate proper air removal and steam penetration
    D. To be able to sterilize the maximum number of instruments simultaneously

14. What is the MOST unique feature of integrating a chemical indicator to the sterilization process?
    A. It performs parallel to biological indicators.
    B. It performs parallel to Bowie-Dick tests.
    C. It makes documentation/record keeping easier.
    D. It ensures highest degree of sterilization.

15. What process does ethylene oxide use to kill microorganisms?
    A. Acidation
    B. Oxidation
    C. Alkylation
    D. Hydration

16. What is the nominal concentration of hydrogen peroxide in a low-temperature gas plasma sterilizer?
    A. 49%
    B. 59%
    C. 69%
    D. 79%

17. When should rigid sterilization containers be biologically tested?
    A. Prior to purchasing
    B. Prior to use
    C. Prior to initial cleaning
    D. Prior to entrance to the facility

18. Which of the following is NOT a factor affecting the dry time of a steam sterilizer?
    A. Type of packaging
    B. Weight of sets
    C. Selected sterilization time
    D. Configuration of the load

19. Ethylene oxide is regulated by all of the following agencies EXCEPT
    A. Occupational Health and Safety Administration
    B. Environmental Protection Agency
    C. Food and Drug Administration
    D. Centers for Disease Control and Prevention

20. Effective sterilization begins with which of the following?
    A. Selection of proper sterilization method
    B. Thorough cleaning
    C. Proper use of instruments by operating room staff
    D. Selection of proper detergent

21. An exhaust hood over the ethylene oxide sterilizer is an example of which of the following?
    A. Engineering control
    B. Biological control
    C. Chemical control
    D. Environmental control

22. Which of the following is the CORRECT incubation temperature range for biological indicators used in steam sterilization?
    A. 131°F - 140°F
    B. 140°F - 183°F
    C. 250°F - 275°F
    D. 270°F - 275°F

23. A chemical indicator responding to two or more critical parameters belongs to which class?
    A. 2
    B. 3
    C. 4
    D. 6

24. How should the pouches be placed when placing paper-plastic pouches in a sterilizer?
    A. Paper facing paper in a basket
    B. Plastic facing plastic in a basket
    C. Paper facing plastic in a basket
    D. Face down in a basket

25. _____ is the MOST effective method of killing microbes?
    A. Ethylene oxide sterilization
    B. Autoclaving
    C. Ozone sterilization
    D. Gas plasma sterilization

KEY (CORRECT ANSWERS)

1.	A	11.	B
2.	C	12.	D
3.	A	13.	C
4.	B	14.	A
5.	A	15.	C
6.	C	16.	B
7.	C	17.	A
8.	B	18.	C
9.	A	19.	D
10.	D	20.	B

21.	A
22.	A
23.	C
24.	C
25.	B

TEST 4

DIRECTIONS: Each question or incomplete statement is followed by several suggested answers or completions. Select the one that BEST answers the question or completes the statement. *PRINT THE LETTER OF THE CORRECT ANSWER IN THE SPACE AT THE RIGHT.*

1. Vials or strips, also known as spore tests, that contain harmless bacterial spores and are used to assess the function of a sterilizer are known as 1.____
    A. chemical indicators B. biological indicators
    C. Bowie-Dick test D. environmental indicators

2. What is the piece of equipment that is used for sterilization through the use of moist heat under pressure? 2.____
    A. Gas plasma sterilizer B. Ozone sterilizer
    C. Ethylene oxide sterilizer D. Autoclave

3. Which of the following is a piece of equipment that is used for sterilization through the use of hot formaldehyde vapors under pressure? 3.____
    A. Autoclave B. Chemical vapor sterilizer
    C. Dry heat sterilizer D. Ozone sterilizer

4. A _____ instrument is an instrument to penetrate soft tissue or bone. 4.____
    A. non-critical B. semi-critical C. critical D. hyper-critical

5. A _____ instrument is an instrument that comes into contact with oral tissues but do not penetrate soft tissue or bone. 5.____
    A. non-critical B. semi-critical C. critical D. hyper-critical

6. A _____ instrument is an instrument that only comes into contact with the skin. 6.____
    A. non-critical B. semi-critical C. critical D. hyper-critical

7. Which of the following is a piece of equipment used for sterilization by means of heated air? 7.____\
    A. Autoclave B. Chemical vapor sterilizer
    C. Dry heat sterilizer D. ozone sterilizer

8. Tapes, strips, and tabs with heat-sensitive chemicals that change color when exposed to certain temperatures are referred to as _____ indicators. 8.____
    A. biological B. environmental
    C. single parameter D. multi-parameter

9. An indicator that reacts to time, temperature, and the presence of steam is referred to as _____ indicators. 9.____
    A. biological B. environmental
    C. single parameter D. multi-parameter

10. In what should instruments be placed if they cannot be processed immediately?   10.____
    A. Saline solution   B. Holding solution
    C. Sterile water   D. Distilled water

11. Use of _____ can prevent the rusting of an instrument.   11.____
    A. sterilants   B. lubricants   C. dessicants   D. disinfectants

12. Where should a process indicator be placed?   12.____
    A. Outside the package   B. Inside the package
    C. On the surface of the instrument   D. Outside the sterilizer

13. Where should a process integrator be placed?   13.____
    A. Outside the package   B. Inside the package
    C. On the surface of the instrument   D. Outside the sterilizer

14. What is the disadvantage to flash sterilization?   14.____
    A. Instruments will rust
    B. Cannot assess bioburden
    C. Inability to wrap items
    D. Don't know the condition of instruments prior to sterilization

15. What is the advantage of chemical vapor sterilization?   15.____
    A. Instruments will not rust.
    B. Instruments can be wrapped
    C. Bioburden easily assessed
    D. Most trustworthy form of sterilization

16. What are the two types of dry heat sterilization?   16.____
    A. Trapped air and cycled air   B. Static air and forced air
    C. Cycled air and static air   D. Forced air and trapped air

17. With what should you rinse instruments that have been processed in a liquid chemical sterilant?   17.____
    A. Alcohol   B. Acetone
    C. Distilled water D. Sterile water

18. What type of sterilization is appropriate for high-speed hand pieces?   18.____
    A. Steam and chemical vapor   B. Ozone and ethylene oxide
    C. Hydrogen peroxide and ozone D. Chemical vapor and ozone

19. High-speed hand pieces should be flushed with _____ to prepare them for sterilization.   19.____
    A. alcohol   B. water
    C. saline   D. acetone

20. What is the preferred method of sterilization for instruments with complex parts, fiber-optics, or camera?   20.____
    A. Dry heat sterilization   B. Chemical sterilization
    C. Low temperature sterilization D. Autoclaving

21. Chemical sterilization qualification of a device requires all of the following EXCEPT _____ testing.
    A. environmental
    B. microbiological
    C. engineering
    D. toxicological

22. Integrating indicators that react to all critical variables with the stated values having been generated to be equivalent to, or exceed, the performance requirements should be assigned to Class
    A. 2
    B. 3
    C. 4
    D. 5

23. What does a negative result for a biological indicator indicate?
    A. Proper sterilization has been met.
    B. Proper sterilization has not been met.
    C. Proper conditions for sterilization have been met.
    D. Proper conditions for sterilization have not been met.

24. Biological indicators should be run with every implant with the exception of which of the following?
    A. Autoclaving
    B. Ethylene oxide
    C. Dry heat
    D. High temperature

25. When moisture comes into contact with ethylene oxide, it forms _____, which is toxic to humans.
    A. ethylene glycol
    B. ethyl alcohol
    C. ethylbenzene
    D. propionaldehyde

KEY (CORRECT ANSWERS)

1.	B	11.	B
2.	D	12.	A
3.	B	13.	B
4.	C	14.	C
5.	B	15.	A
6.	A	16.	B
7.	C	17.	D
8.	C	18.	A
9.	D	19.	B
10.	B	20.	C

21.	A
22.	D
23.	C
24.	B
25.	A

EXAMINATION SECTION
TEST 1

DIRECTIONS: Each question or incomplete statement is followed by several suggested answers or completions. Select the one that BEST answers the question or completes the statement. *PRINT THE LETTER OF THE CORRECT ANSWER IN THE SPACE AT THE RIGHT.*

1. Kerrison Laminectomy Rongeurs should be tested using which of the following?
   A. Tissue paper
   B. Index card
   C. Rubber testing material
   D. Plastic dowel rod

2. Which of the following is NOT an acceptable form of instrument marking?
   A. Laser-etching
   B. Acid-based etching
   C. Heat-infused nylon
   D. Electric etching

3. Scissors with tungsten carbide cutting edges are usually identified by what color?
   A. Gold   B. Black   C. Silver   D. Red

4. What is the purpose of a suction stylet?
   A. Facilitate the sterilization process
   B. Provide a measuring guide for the surgeon
   C. Unclog the suction during surgery
   D. Facilitate blood flow during surgical procedures

5. Endoscopes are often processed in a mechanical unit known as
   A. ultrasonic cleaner
   B. washer-decontaminator
   C. automatic endoscope reprocessor
   D. flush-pulse endoscope reprocessor

6. What is the FIRST step to inspect the insulation of a laparascopic instrument?
   A. Check the collar at the distal tip
   B. Attempt to slide the insulation back
   C. Check the handle for chipping or cracking
   D. Check the collar at the proximal tip

7. Which of the following statements are TRUE regarding endoscopes?
   A. Not all endoscopes can be processed in an automatic endoscopic reprocessor.
   B. Ultrasonic cleaning is the process of choice for endoscopes.
   C. All endoscopes should be steam sterilized.
   D. Flexible endoscopes are not easily damaged.

8. What should be the FIRST step when processing flexible endoscopes?
   A. High level sterilization
   B. Manual cleaning
   C. Leak testing
   D. Drying

9. Which endoscope would be dispensed for a procedure that required visualization of the lower part of the large intestine?
   A. Colonoscope
   B. Sigmoidoscope
   C. Ureteroscope
   D. Gastroscope

10. What is the purpose of using a decontamination battery or cord when cleaning powered surgical instruments?
    A. To keep fluid from entering the unit
    B. To keep functioning batteries and cords clean
    C. To prevent electrical shock
    D. To test the unit while cleaning

11. Who should provide information regarding cleaning processes for endoscopes?
    A. Hospital policies
    B. Endoscope manufacturer
    C. Society of Gastroenterology Nurses and Associates
    D. Association for Professionals in Infection Control and Epidemiology

12. Where should electronic testing of laparoscopic insulation be performed?
    A. In the contamination area prior to cleaning
    B. In the operating room at the end of the procedure
    C. At the factory or onsite repair unit
    D. In the clean assembly area prior to set assembly

13. What substance should be used to thoroughly rinse all traces of disinfectant from the channels of an endoscope?
    A. Filtered water
    B. Forced air
    C. Water containing approved sterilant
    D. Heated gluteraldehyde

14. Which of the following statements is TRUE regarding loaner instruments?
    A. They should be decontaminated prior to use.
    B. They should never be used.
    C. They should be sterilized using a low temperature process.
    D. They should be decontaminated only if they appear to be soiled.

15. Which of the following common items of patient care equipment limits the development of deep vein thrombosis and peripheral edema in immobile patients?
    A. Respirator
    B. Intermittent suction device
    C. Sequential compression unit
    D. Defibrillator

16. Where is patient care equipment typically stored?
    A. On patient units
    B. In sterile storage areas
    C. In the Central Service Department
    D. In the Biomedical Engineering Department

17. When patient equipment enters a healthcare facility, who has the responsibility of checking it prior to patient use?
    A. Biomedical Technician
    B. Central Service Technician
    C. Central Service Director
    D. Infection Control Committee Member

17.____

18. Which of the following is TRUE regarding tracking of patient care equipment?
    A. Tracking patient care equipment can prevent equipment shortages.
    B. Tracking of patient care equipment requires a computer.
    C. Patient care equipment should only be tracked if it has a value in excess of an amount specified by the facility.
    D. Patient care equipment should only be tracked if its usage will be charged to the patients.

18.____

19. When should equipment be inspected for obvious hazards such as cracked or frayed electrical cords?
    A. Prior to patient use
    B. During preventative maintenance activities
    C. When there are complaints from user department personnel
    D. When the equipment is being cleaned

19.____

20. Which piece of legislation requires that the healthcare facility report malfunctions of medical devices that have contributed to patient injury, illness and/or death to the manufacturer and the FDA?
    A. Safe Medical Devices Act   B. FDA Equipment Notification Act
    C. EPA Patient Security Act   D. OSHA Patient Safety Act

20.____

21. All patient care equipment that is dispensed for use must be considered _____ and handled as such regardless of its appearance.
    A. clean   B. sterile   C. visibly soiled   D. contaminated

21.____

22. Which hospital department employs technicians that perform safety inspections and functional tests on equipment?
    A. Maintenance   B. Biomedical Engineering
    C. Materials Management   D. Infection Control

22.____

23. Which agency requires preventative maintenance standards be established for medical equipment?
    A. Joint Commission
    B. Occupational Safety and Health Administration
    C. Association of PeriOperative Registered Nurses
    D. Association for the Advancement of Medical Instrumentation

23.____

24. Which of the following statements is TRUE regarding disposable components such as pads and tubing on patient care equipment?
They such be
   A. discarded at point of use
   B. discarded during preventative maintenance
   C. reprocessed for re-use
   D. removed in the Biomedical Engineering Department

25. What should occur if an equipment malfunction causes harm to patients?
Equipment should be
   A. discarded immediately
   B. sequestered for inspection by OSHA personnel
   C. sent to the manufacturer for repairs
   D. returned immediately to the Biomedical Department

KEY (CORRECT ANSWERS)

1.	B		11.	B
2.	D		12.	D
3.	A		13.	A
4.	C		14.	A
5.	C		15.	C
6.	A		16.	D
7.	A		17.	A
8.	C		18.	B
9.	B		19.	D
10.	A		20.	D

21. D
22. C
23. B
24. A
25. D

TEST 2

DIRECTIONS: Each question or incomplete statement is followed by several suggested answers or completions. Select the one that BEST answers the question or completes the statement. *PRINT THE LETTER OF THE CORRECT ANSWER IN THE SPACE AT THE RIGHT.*

1. What is the difference between equipment leasing and equipment rental? 1.____
   A. Equipment leasing is an operating expense; equipment rental does not have cost implications.
   B. Leasing involves purchase; rental does not require ownership.
   C. Equipment rental is usually done on a shorter-term basis than equipment leasing.
   D. Equipment leasing involves the most expensive equipment; equipment rental involves less expensive equipment.

2. In what condition should patient care equipment be stored? 2.____
   A. Ready to clean
   B. Ready to inspect
   C. Ready to sterilize
   D. Ready to use

3. Which of the following statements is TRUE regarding preventative maintenance for patient care equipment? 3.____
   A. It is designed to identify potential problems before they occur.
   B. It is designed to be performed when a piece of equipment injures a patient.
   C. It is performed when user unit notices a problem.
   D. It is performed by Central Service prior to the equipment being dispensed.

4. What can result from laparoscopic instrument insulation failure? 4.____
   A. Cuts   B. Scrapes   C. Burns   D. Bruises

5. The purpose of a decontamination battery is to protect from _____ invasion. 5.____
   A. dust   B. fluid   C. prion   D. bacterial

6. Which of the following is NOT an appropriate power source for powered surgical instruments? 6.____
   A. Air   B. Battery   C. Electricity   D. Solar

7. What type of endoscope allows for visual inspection of the upper digestive tract? 7.____
   A. Gastroscope
   B. Bronchoscope
   C. Sigmoidoscope
   D. Cystoscope

8. What type of endoscope allows for visual inspection of the urethra and the bladder? 8.____
   A. Sigmoidoscope
   B. Cystoscope
   C. Bronchoscope
   D. Colonoscope

9. What type of endoscope allows for visualization of the tracheobronchial tree?
   A. Cystoscope
   B. Sigmoidoscope
   C. Gastroscope
   D. Broncoscope

10. What type of endoscope allows for visualization of the entire large intestine?
    A. Colonoscope
    B. Gastroscope
    C. Sigmoidoscope
    D. Cystoscope

11. What powered surgical instrument is used for driving very small wires through bone?
    A. Sternal saw   B. Cebatome   C. Dermatome   D. Micro Drill

12. What powered surgical instrument would be used for open heart surgery?
    A. Dermabrader   B. Sternal saw   C. Cebatome   D. Micro Drill

13. What powered surgical instrument is used to remove cement?
    A. Dermatome   B. Cebatome   C. Dental Drill   D. Micro Drill

14. What powered surgical instrument would be used to harvest skin grafts and reshape skin surfaces?
    A. Dermatome   B. Cebatome   C. Sternal Saw   D. Micro Drill

15. Which piece of equipment would be used to perform specific cutting actions such as reciprocating or oscillating?
    A. Scissors   B. Forceps   C. Saw   D. Retractors

16. Which surgical instrument would be used to cut, incise, or dissect tissue?
    A. Retractors   B. Scissors   C. Saw   D. Forceps

17. Prolonged exposure to which common operating room substance can result in damage to instruments?
    A. Betadine
    B. Alcohol
    C. Deionized water
    D. Saline solution

18. Which of the following surgical instruments would be used to grasp?
    A. Forceps   B. Retractors   C. Cebatome   D. Dermatone

19. What is the part of a ring-handled instrument where the two parts meet and pivot?
    A. Box lock   B. Joint lock   C. Hinge lock   D. Bolt lock

20. Tissue forceps have _____ and dressing forceps have _____.
    A. serrations; teeth
    B. teeth; serrations
    C. rubber tips; steel tips
    D. steel tips; rubber tips

21. Which type of stainless steel, also known as 400 series stainless steel, can be heat-hardened and used for the manufacturing of surgical instruments?
    A. Ferritic stainless steel
    B. Austenitic stainless steel
    C. Martensitic stainless steel
    D. Precipitation hardened steel

22. What piece of surgical equipment is a self-retaining retractor? 22.____
    A. Rongeurs   B. Gelpi   C. Ratchet   D. Cannulas

23. Which part of a ring-handled instrument locks the handles in place? 23.____
    A. Box lock   B. Ratchet   C. Joint lock   D. Gelpi

24. What piece of surgical equipment is used to cut away bone and tissue? 24.____
    A. Saw   B. Scissors   C. Rongeurs   D. Forceps

25. What is the chemical process that is applied during the manufacturing of surgical instruments that provides a corrosion-resistant finish by forming a thin, transparent oxide film? 25.____
    A. Sterilization   B. Cavitation
    C. Passivation   D. Decontamination

KEY (CORRECT ANSWERS)

1.	B	11.	D
2.	D	12.	B
3.	A	13.	B
4.	C	14.	A
5.	B	15.	C
6.	D	16.	B
7.	A	17.	D
8.	B	18.	A
9.	D	19.	A
10.	A	20.	B

21. C
22. B
23. B
24. C
25. C

TEST 3

DIRECTIONS: Each question or incomplete statement is followed by several suggested answers or completions. Select the one that BEST answers the question or completes the statement. *PRINT THE LETTER OF THE CORRECT ANSWER IN THE SPACE AT THE RIGHT.*

1. Which of the following is a surgical instrument with a hollow barrel through the center?
   A. Cannulas   B. Retractors   C. Rongeurs   D. Gelpi

   1.____

2. Which of the following is the internal path through a needle, tube, or surgical instrument?
   A. Cannulas   B. Lumen   C. Catheter   D. Tunnel

   2.____

3. What is the MOST corrosion-resistant form of stainless steel?
   A. Austenitic stainless steels
   B. Ferritic stainless steels
   C. Precipitation hardened stainless steels
   D. Martensitic stainless steels

   3.____

4. What is the proper method for cleaning fiber-optic light cables?
   A. In the autoclave
   B. Soft cloth and detergent
   C. Vigorous scraping
   D. Hydrogen peroxide and rinsed with distilled water

   4.____

5. The mechanical action in the ultra cleaning process that uses sound waves and imploding bubbles is called
   A. passivation   B. cavitation
   C. sterilization   D. decontamination

   5.____

6. Which piece of equipment is an example of a flexible endoscope?
   A. Cystoscope   B. Cavitation
   C. Arthroscope   D. Resectoscope

   6.____

7. Which piece of equipment is used to regulate body temperature?
   A. Sequential compression device   B. Cebatome
   C. Dermatome   D. Hypo/Hyperthermia machine

   7.____

8. _____ compression devices are used to prevent the formation of blood clots.
   A. Sequential   B. Standardized
   C. Sterilized   D. Subcutaneous

   8.____

9. What is the appropriate grade of stainless steel used to manufacture osteotomes?
   A. 200 Grade   B. 300 Grade   C. 400 Grade   D. 500 Grade

   9.____

10. For manual lubrication, surgical instruments should be placed in a lubricant solution and then
    A. sterilized
    B. autoclaved
    C. wiped clean
    D. room air-dried

10._____

11. It is appropriate to use dissecting scissors to cut
    A. dressings   B. bone   C. wire   D. tissue

11._____

12. The purpose of the tungsten carbine insert on a needle holder is to _____ the suture needle better.
    A. guide   B. place   C. maneuver   D. hold

12._____

13. What piece of equipment is used to artificially stimulate the venous plantar plexus in order to increase circulation of bed-ridden patients?
    A. Defibrillator
    B. Foot pump
    C. Sequential pressure device
    D. Pacemaker

13._____

14. Which piece of equipment applies a brief electroshock to restore the rhythm of the heart?
    A. Pacemaker   B. Defibrillator   C. Metabolizer   D. Retractor

14._____

15. An emergency eyewash station must be which of the following?
    A. Completely automated
    B. Hands-on operated
    C. Hands-free operated
    D. Manually operated

15._____

16. Which organization has established standards for the effective processing of flexible endoscopes?
    A. Society of Gastroenterology Nurses and Associates
    B. Association for Professionals in Infection Control and Epidemiology
    C. Association of PeriOperative Registered Nurses
    D. Association for the Advancement of Medical Instrumentation

16._____

17. Instruments with lumens should be soaked in what position?
    A. Horizontal
    B. Vertical
    C. At a 30° angle
    D. At a 45° angle

17._____

18. Automatic washers clean using spray-force action called
    A. containment
    B. impalement
    C. impingement
    D. enforcement

18._____

19. Which piece of equipment allows the patient to self-administer pain medication?
    A. Foot pump
    B. Sequential pressure device
    C. Heart pump
    D. Patient controlled analgesia pump

19._____

20. Which of the following statements is TRUE regarding powered surgical instruments?
    A. Hoses that attach to pneumatic-powered instruments should not be sterilized.
    B. Cables should be disconnected from the handpiece during processing.
    C. Powered surgical instruments should be completely disassembled prior to processing.
    D. It is important that fluid does not enter the cable or handpiece during processing.

21. The decision to sterilize or high-level disinfect an endoscope is based according to which classification system?
    A. Nightingale
    B. Spaulding
    C. Schrodinger
    D. Federal Medical Device

22. What type of fire extinguisher is appropriate to be used on flammable objects?
    A. Type A
    B. Type B
    C. Type C
    D. Type D

23. Microgrind or Supercut scissors are usually identified by what color handle?
    A. Black
    B. Blue
    C. Silver
    D. Red

24. An ionsufflator blows what gas into the patient's abdominal cavity in order to extend the laparoscope and allow the surgeon to view the patient's internal organs?
    A. Carbon monoxide
    B. Carbon dioxide
    C. Nitric oxide
    D. Helium nitride

25. At what pressure does the insufflator blow gasses into the abdominal cavity?
    A. 5mmHg – 8 mmHg
    B. 9mmHg – 11mmHg
    C. 12mmHg – 15mmHg
    D. 16mmHg – 19mmHg

KEY (CORRECT ANSWERS)

1. A
2. B
3. A
4. B
5. B

6. B
7. D
8. A
9. C
10. D

11. D
12. D
13. B
14. B
15. C

16. A
17. B
18. C
19. D
20. A

21. B
22. B
23. A
24. B
25. C

TEST 4

DIRECTIONS: Each question or incomplete statement is followed by several suggested answers or completions. Select the one that BEST answers the question or completes the statement. *PRINT THE LETTER OF THE CORRECT ANSWER IN THE SPACE AT THE RIGHT.*

1. What do many laparoscopic instruments have to deliver electrosurgical energy to the distal end of the instrument?
    A. Insulation
    B. Tungsten carbide tips
    C. Cautery posts
    D. Defibrillators
    1.____

2. What part of a laparoscope is NOT used for access or exposure of a surgical site?
    A. Cautery post
    B. Camera
    C. Light source
    D. Insufflator
    2.____

3. Which of the following is used to transmit light in a laparoscope to the surgical site?
    A. Electricity
    B. Fiber-optic cables
    C. Microwaves
    D. Ultrasonic waves
    3.____

4. What type of light sources could be connected to the laparoscope with a cable?
    A. Helium and neon
    B. Argon and neon
    C. Halogen and xenon
    D. Argon and xenon
    4.____

5. Laparoscopic equipment that is NOT part of the sterile field is decontaminated as part of what process?
    A. Room cleaning
    B. Instrument cleaning
    C. Sterilization
    D. Ionization
    5.____

6. After they are disassembled, what should be used to wipe blood from the outer surfaces on non-immersible items?
    A. Hydrogen peroxide
    B. Sterile water
    C. Alcohol
    D. Betadine
    6.____

7. Which of the following should be used to assist cleaning of box-locks, serrations, and other crevices?
    A. Wire-bristled brush
    B. Soft-bristled brush
    C. Sterile towel
    D. Sterile gauze
    7.____

8. Instruments should be kept under the solution while cleaning to avoid the creation of
    A. contaminants
    B. condensation
    C. aerosols
    D. prions
    8.____

9. Because it is inserted blindly, which part of the laparoscope can cause injuries to blood vessels and organs if it is inserted too far?
   A. Trocar
   B. Camera
   C. Fiber-optic cables
   D. Insufflator

10. The _____ optic surface is NOT one of the optical areas to clean on a laparoscope.
    A. internal
    B. distal
    C. fiber
    D. proximal

11. What is the minimum amount of time that is required for flushing the internal channel of a laparoscope to allow for adequate removal of organic debris?
    A. 10 seconds
    B. 20 seconds
    C. 30 seconds
    D. 40 seconds

12. What may be an indication that some of the fibers are broken in a laparoscope?
    A. Cracked appearance
    B. Double vision
    C. Appearance of black dots
    D. Over-illumination

13. Any bare metal, where there should be insulation, can cause electrical _____ during the surgical procedure and potentially burn vital organs inside the patient but outside the view of the surgeon.
    A. arcing
    B. avalanching
    C. adversity
    D. advancement

14. Which of the following is TRUE regarding ergonomic injuries?
    A. Not a concern for Central Service employees
    B. Are a risk factor for persons who perform repetitive or physical work
    C. Are rare in today's work environment
    D. Only occur in an office setting

15. Which of the following is TRUE regarding secondary containers of chemicals?
    A. Must be labeled with a permanent marker and must state the name of the chemical and designated storage location.
    B. There are no restrictions regarding secondary container labels.
    C. Must be labeled with a copy of the original manufacturer's label or a generic label that identifies hazard warnings and directions.
    D. Secondary containers of chemicals are forbidden in healthcare facilities.

16. What is burning in a Class C fire?
    A. Wood or paper
    B. Cloth or plastic
    C. Flammable liquid
    D. Energized electrical equipment

17. Which of the following is NOT required to ensure sharps safety?
    A. Never use your fingers to remove a blade from a scalpel.
    B. Wash all disposable sharps prior to discarding them.
    C. Separate reusable sharps in an appropriate container.
    D. Dispose all single use sharps in an appropriate container.

18. What process will help instrument identification tape adhere to the instrument?
    A. Passivation
    B. Cavitation
    C. Autoclaving
    D. Decontamination

19. Heart valves and pacemakers are examples of what class of medical device by the Food and Drug Administration?
    A. Class I
    B. Class II
    C. Class III
    D. Class IV

20. Class III medical devices are classified by the Food and Drug Administration as _____ risk.
    A. no
    B. low
    C. intermediate
    D. high

21. Failure to receive accreditation from the Joint Commission can result in the facility's loss of
    A. patients
    B. privileges
    C. Medicare reimbursement
    D. physicians

22. Which agency imposes very strict labeling requirements on manufacturers of chemicals used by the Central Service Department?
    A. Food and Drug Administration
    B. Environmental Protection Agency
    C. Occupational Safety and Health Administration
    D. Centers for Disease Control and Prevention

23. Which agency is responsible for administering regulations under the Clean Air Act?
    A. Environmental Protection Agency
    B. Food and Drug Administration
    C. Association of PeriOperative Registered Nurses
    D. Association for the Advancement of Medical Instrumentation

24. Which organization sets recommended practices and standards for care and processing of medical devices and systems?
    A. Association of PeriOperative Registered Nurses
    B. Association for the Advancement of Medical Instrumentation
    C. Society of Gastroenterology Nurses and Associates
    D. Association for Professionals in Infection Control and Epidemiology

25. Which of the following substances break down blood, mucous, feces, and albumin?
    A. Lipase
    B. Protease enzymes
    C. Surfactant
    D. Ethylene oxide

KEY (CORRECT ANSWERS)

1.	C	11.	B
2.	A	12.	C
3.	B	13.	A
4.	C	14.	B
5.	A	15.	D
6.	B	16.	D
7.	B	17.	B
8.	C	18.	C
9.	A	19.	C
10.	A	20.	D

21.	C
22.	B
23.	A
24.	B
25.	B

EXAMINATION SECTION

TEST 1

DIRECTIONS: Each question or incomplete statement is followed by several suggested answers or completions. Select the one that BEST answers the question or completes the statement. *PRINT THE LETTER OF THE CORRECT ANSWER IN THE SPACE AT THE RIGHT.*

1. The inventory system that stocks supplies by pre-determined stock levels is known as a(n) ____ system.
   A. exchange B. case cart C. par-level D. pick-n-pak

2. _____ is defined as the movement of supplies throughout the healthcare facilities.
   A. Procurement
   B. Distribution
   C. Acquisition
   D. Inventory management

3. The inventory system in which items are ordered in larger quantities, such as by the case instead of individually, as a cost containment measure is referred to as a(n)
   A. exchange system
   B. case cart system
   C. par-level system
   D. economic order quantity

4. Which of the following statements are TRUE regarding official inventory?
   A. It can be counted as an asset on the facility's balance sheet.
   B. It is owned by the vendor, but stored at the healthcare facility.
   C. It is owned by the healthcare facility, but stored by the vendor.
   D. It is no longer present in modern healthcare facilities.

5. The _____ system uses two identical carts to facilitate supply replenishment.
   A. requisition
   B. par-level
   C. exchange cart
   D. case cart

6. Which inventory system is characterized by the items being owned by the vendor but stored at the healthcare facility?
   A. Requisition
   B. Consignment
   C. Par-level
   D. Procurement

7. Which inventory system is characterized by the facility keeping minimal stock on hand and supplies are delivered as needed?
   A. Consignment
   B. Procurement
   C. Just-in-time
   D. Par-level

8. Which inventory system provides supplies and instruments for individual surgical procedures?
   A. Case cart
   B. Just-in-time
   C. Exchange cart
   D. Requisition

9. The recommended number of air exchanges for the clean/sterile storage area of the Central Service Department is _____ air exchanges/hour.
   A. 2   B. 4   C. 6   D. 8

10. The recommended humidity level for the clean/sterile storage area of the Central Service Department is less than
    A. 50%   B. 60%   C. 70%   D. 80%

11. Open wire racks used in the sterile storage area should have what kind of bottom?
    A. Wire   B. Porous   C. Solid   D. Bottomless

12. How often should the floors of the Central Service Department be wet mopped?
    A. Hourly
    B. Once per shift
    C. Daily
    D. Weekly

13. The _____ system is a method of inventory distribution in which item needs are requested by the user department and filled from a central storage location.
    A. case cart
    B. just-in-time
    C. exchange cart
    D. requisition

14. When a perpetual inventory system is used, the difference between the amount of supply that should be available and the amount that is actually available is known as
    A. volume
    B. variance
    C. displacement
    D. loss

15. The _____ method of stock rotation ensures that the older materials are used first.
    A. revolving
    B. FIFO
    C. requisition
    D. just-in-time

16. What is the minimum amount of time that packaging materials should be held at room temperature and at 35-70% relative humidity prior to sterilization?
    A. 2 hours   B. 4 hours   C. 6 hours   D. 8 hours

17. Which of the following is a flat wrapping technique that applies one wrap on top of another to create a package within a package?
    A. Double-wrap
    B. Pouching
    C. Crossover
    D. Sequential

18. Which agency is responsible for regulating sterilization packaging material?
    A. Occupational Safety and Health Administration
    B. Food and Drug Administration
    C. Centers for Disease Control and Prevention
    D. National Institute of Health

19. Which type of packaging contains no cellulosic materials and would be used to package small items for low temperature sterilization?
    A. Spunbonded polyolefin   B. Kraft paper
    C. Surgical drapes   D. Sterile towels

19.____

20. _____ is a type of packaging that can be used in dry heat sterilization but is not recommended for other types of sterilization.
    A. Kraft paper   B. Spunbonded polyolefin
    C. Surgical drapes   D. Aluminum foil

20.____

21. Package content information should always be written on which side of the paper/plastic pouches?
    A. Paper   B. Plastic   C. Visible   D. Non-visible

21.____

22. The recommended maximum density, per cubic foot, in a linen pack is _____ lbs.
    A. 4.4   B. 5.8   C. 7.2   D. 8.6

22.____

23. The weight of wrapped basin sets should NOT exceed how much?
    A. 5 lbs.   B. 7 lbs.   C. 9 lbs.   D. 11 lbs.

23.____

24. Which of the following occurs when consumable or reusable inventory items are not available when needed?
    A. Close outs B. Stock outs   C. Phase outs   D. Fall outs

24.____

25. When items are needed immediately, or at once, Central Service Technicians may receive what kind of order?
    A. STAT   B. Critical   C. Emergent   D. Pronto

25.____

KEY (CORRECT ANSWERS)

1.	C	11.	C
2.	B	12.	C
3.	D	13.	D
4.	A	14.	B
5.	C	15.	B
6.	B	16.	A
7.	C	17.	D
8.	A	18.	B
9.	B	19.	A
10.	C	20.	D

21.	B
22.	C
23.	B
24.	B
25.	A

TEST 2

DIRECTIONS: Each question or incomplete statement is followed by several suggested answers or completions. Select the one that BEST answers the question or completes the statement. *PRINT THE LETTER OF THE CORRECT ANSWER IN THE SPACE AT THE RIGHT.*

1. The number of times that inventory is purchased, consumed, and replaced is called inventory _____ rate.
   A. reorder   B. turnover   C. depletion   D. replenishment

   1.____

2. Something of value that is owned by an organization or a person is referred to as an
   A. asset   B. goods   C. possession   D. item

   2.____

3. Products such as detergents, sterilization quality control assurance products, and other items that are purchased, used up, and replaced are known as _____ inventory.
   A. reusable   B. official   C. consumable   D. turnover

   3.____

4. Items such as sterilizers, mechanical washers, and other expensive items are examples of _____ equipment.
   A. common use   B. freestanding
   C. authorized   D. capital

   4.____

5. The inventory management strategy that pays the most attention to the items with the highest dollar value and less attention to items with the lowest dollar amount is referred to as _____ analysis.
   A. cost   B. inventory   C. 123   D. ABC

   5.____

6. The act of withdrawing supplies from storage for transfer to the areas where they will be used is called
   A. distribution   B. delivery   C. issue   D. resourcing

   6.____

7. A(n) _____ system is a computerized system that allows clinical staff to obtain patient items from a storage unit on the user unit. When the item is removed, the clinical staff keys in a code or uses a scan to account for the items they are removing. That data is compiled by the computer and at an established time, an order is generated to restock the storage unit?
   A. par-level
   B. exchange cart
   C. case cart
   D. Automated Supply Replenishment

   7.____

8. If the operating room places a requisition for 100 items and only 76 of the items can be filled, the inventory service level is _____ and the stock out rate is _____.
   A. 24%; 76%   B. 76%; 24%   C. 38%; 62%   D. 62%; 38%

   8.____

9. Which department is responsible for checking and maintaining patient care equipment for safety and function?
   A. Maintenance Department
   B. Medical Technology
   C. Electrical Engineering
   D. Biomedical Engineering

10. What type of system uses small bandage-sized transponders that provide real-time data about the location of a specific piece of equipment?
    A. Radio frequency identification system
    B. Automated supply replenishment system
    C. Case cart system
    D. Just-in-time system

11. Handwritten tags, wall-mounted bulletin boards and log books are examples of what type of tracking system?
    A. Universal   B. Professional   C. Managerial   D. Manual

12. Nurses, physicians and other professionals working in the healthcare facility are _____ customers of Central Service.
    A. external   B. priority   C. internal   D. administrative

13. Central Service should be capable of planning for approximately what percentage of the total needs of a unit?
    A. 50%   B. 75%   C. 90%   D. 100%

14. Which of the following must be made available to all distribution personnel?
    A. Policies and procedures for correct handling of sterile supplies
    B. Computerized inventory and distribution systems
    C. A detailed map of the healthcare facility
    D. Dedicated locker room

15. Which of the following is another name for par-level inventory?
    A. Automatically replenished inventory
    B. Volume adjusted inventory
    C. Fixed inventory level
    D. Department specific inventory

16. Which of the following is considered a disadvantage of an exchange cart system?
    A. Supplies can potentially outdate.
    B. Patients are charged immediately.
    C. Supplies must be requisitioned.
    D. Inventory is duplicated.

17. For what reason should watches and other jewelry not be worn in the Central Service Area?
    A. They can get caught in a sterilizer.
    B. They can be easily broken.
    C. They harbor bacteria.
    D. They could be damaged by the chemicals.

18. What is the MAIN theory behind the use of standard precautions?
    A. Patients may be at risk for infection whether they have officially been diagnosed or not.
    B. Patients in high risk categories may be infectious.
    C. Patients diagnosed with specific diseases may be infectious.
    D. You may be infectious and could transmit to the patient.

18._____

19. The absence of microorganisms that cause disease is referred to as
    A. infection protection
    B. infection control
    C. sepsis
    D. asepsis

19._____

20. Which of the following is the LARGEST customer for the Central Service Department?
    A. Intensive Car Unit
    B. Coronary Care Unit
    C. Operating Room
    D. Emergency Room

20._____

21. How many times should instrument marking tape be wrapped around a device?
    A. 1 – 1.5 times
    B. 1.5 – 2 times
    C. 2 – 2.5 times
    D. 2.5 – 3 times

21._____

22. Which of the following is an example of regulated medical waste?
    A. Discarded sterilization wraps
    B. Blood-soaked sponges
    C. General trash from the Operating Room
    D. Saline-soaked gauze

22._____

23. Which of the following is NOT included on an MSDS sheet?
    A. Special precautions
    B. Product identification
    C. Product flammability
    D. Required inventory levels

23._____

24. Which of the following statements is TRUE regarding patient care equipment tracking?
    A. Tracking patient care equipment can prevent equipment shortages.
    B. Tracking patient care equipment can be the cause of equipment shortages.
    C. Patient care equipment tracking requires a computer.
    D. Patient care equipment must only be tracked if its usage will be charged to patients.

24._____

25. The temperature in the sterile storage area should NOT exceed
    A. 68°F
    B. 70°F
    C. 72°F
    D. 75°F

25._____

KEY (CORRECT ANSWERS)

1.	B	11.	D
2.	A	12.	C
3.	C	13.	C
4.	D	14.	A
5.	D	15.	C
6.	C	16.	D
7.	D	17.	C
8.	B	18.	A
9.	D	19.	D
10.	A	20.	D

21. A
22. B
23. D
24. A
25. D

TEST 3

DIRECTIONS: Each question or incomplete statement is followed by several suggested answers or completions. Select the one that BEST answers the question or completes the statement. *PRINT THE LETTER OF THE CORRECT ANSWER IN THE SPACE AT THE RIGHT.*

1. Sterile items that are protected from the environment have been proven to remain sterile for
   A. 6 months
   B. 1 year
   C. 5 years
   D. indefinitely

   1.____

2. The period of time during which a sterile item is considered safe to use is referred to as
   A. expiration date
   B. shelf life
   C. half life
   D. exposure time

   2.____

3. Which of the following factors is a reason for a manufacturer to assign an expiration date to a sterile medical device?
   A. Product degradation
   B. Cost of the product
   C. Product labeling
   D. Type of sterilization method

   3.____

4. How often should a package be visually inspected for integrity?
   A. Hourly
   B. Prior to use
   C. Daily
   D. Every time it is handled

   4.____

5. Sterile trays that may be subjected to storage challenges should be placed in sterility
   A. standby
   B. holding area
   C. maintenance
   D. collection

   5.____

6. Stock rotation and frequent evaluation of stock levels will minimize the need for reprocessing and prevent
   A. overuse
   B. misuse
   C. unauthorized allocation
   D. outdates

   6.____

7. What should be done if a reusable sterile basin set is dropped on the floor?
   A. No action required
   B. It should be immediately disposed
   C. It should be sent to be reprocessed
   D. It should be used in a non-sterile environment

   7.____

8. The sterile storage area should be located _____ sterilization.
   A. opposite to
   B. adjacent to
   C. within
   D. beneath

   8.____

9. With what instrument can humidity be measured?
   A. Hygrometer
   B. Thermometer
   C. Manometer
   D. Cryometer

   9.____

69

10. Shelving in the sterile storage area must be kept at what distance from the outside walls?
    A. 2 inches   B. 4 inches   C. 6 inches   D. 8 inches

11. Shelving in the sterile storage area must be kept at what distance from the ceiling and/or sprinkler heads?
    A. 6 inches   B. 12 inches   C. 18 inches   D. 24 inches

12. Why is it important to control humidity in the sterile storage area?
    A. To prevent equipment malfunction
    B. To prevent the growth of microorganisms
    C. To maintain a comfortable work environment
    D. To prevent instrument corrosion

13. When placing ring-handled instruments in an instrument tray, which of the following is TRUE?
    A. Unlock the handles and open the instruments
    B. Arrange the instruments in the order of their use
    C. Arrange the instruments in alphabetical order
    D. Lock the handles to prevent damage during sterilization

14. Which of the following is NOT a reason for tracking supplies, equipment, and instruments?
    A. Ensure items can be located quickly
    B. Measure item usage
    C. Meet CDC and OSHA requirements
    D. Assist with quality processes

15. Which of the following is NOT a feature of an instrument tracking system?
    A. Product updates and recall information
    B. Productivity information
    C. Financial data
    D. Quality assurance information

16. Which is defined as giving control of a hospital's equipment management system to an external entity?
    A. Insourcing   B. Outsourcing   C. Delegating   D. Collaborating

17. Which of the following is a major cause of contamination of sterile items?
    A. Moisture   B. Dust   C. Air pressure   D. Insects

18. Only what group of people should enter the central storage area?
    A. Hospital administrators   B. Nurses
    C. Physicians   D. Authorized personnel

19. _____ should never be allowed in either a clean storage area or a sterile storage area and should never be used as storage containers in these areas.
    A. Porous containers   B. Solid bottom containers
    C. Shipping cartons   D. Wicking materials

20. Which of the following is the desired storage method for sterile items?
    A. Open shelving
    B. Dedicated storage room
    C. Common hospital storage
    D. Cabinet storage

21. Freshly sterilized items should be thoroughly _____ before storage.
    A. rinsed   B. dried   C. cooled   D. packaged

22. Contact between hot items and a cool surface will cause formation of _____ on packaging and hence contaminate the package contents.
    A. pathogens
    B. condensation
    C. spores
    D. biofilm

23. In order to provide maximum protection of sterile items from contamination, what should be used to overwrap hospital sterilized packages?
    A. Dust cover
    B. Sterile drape
    C. Sterile towel
    D. Sterile sheet

24. What is the proper thickness of a dust cover?
    A. 1 mm – 2 mm
    B. 2 mm – 3 mm
    C. 3 mm – 4 mm
    D. 4 mm – 5 mm

25. Which of the following is NOT compensated for by a dust cover EXCEPT improper
    A. environmental conditions
    B. storage techniques
    C. handling procedures
    D. sterilization method

KEY (CORRECT ANSWERS)

1.	D	11.	C
2.	B	12.	B
3.	A	13.	A
4.	D	14.	C
5.	C	15.	A
6.	D	16.	B
7.	C	17.	A
8.	B	18.	D
9.	A	19.	C
10.	A	20.	D

21.	C
22.	B
23.	A
24.	B
25.	D

TEST 4

DIRECTIONS: Each question or incomplete statement is followed by several suggested answers or completions. Select the one that BEST answers the question or completes the statement. *PRINT THE LETTER OF THE CORRECT ANSWER IN THE SPACE AT THE RIGHT.*

1. Which of the following is NOT a recommended method for cleaning the floor of the sterile storage area?
   A. Dry mopped
   B. Wet mopped
   C. Wet-vacuumed
   D. Scrubbed with germicidal solution

    1.____

2. How often should storage shelving and containers be damp dusted?
   A. Hourly
   B. Daily
   C. Weekly
   D. Routinely as needed

    2.____

3. Surfaces should be thoroughly _____ after cleaning and placing supplies back on the shelves.
   A. rinsed
   B. dried
   C. cooled
   D. packaged

    3.____

4. What is the MOST common method for identifying the shelf life of an item?
   A. Manufactured date
   B. Sterilized date
   C. Packaged date
   D. Shipping date

    4.____

5. Generally, commercial items that have a fixed shelf life contain which of the following substances?
   A. Chlorides and nitrates
   B. Pharmaceuticals and latex
   C. Calcium and magnesium
   D. hydrogen peroxide and acetone

    5.____

6. Sterility is _____ related.
   A. event
   B. time
   C. user
   D. patient

    6.____

7. The sterile storage should be under _____ pressure in relation to adjacent areas.
   A. negative
   B. positive
   C. neutral
   D. zeror

    7.____

8. How often should walls, ceilings, vents, and ceiling fixtures be damp dusted?
   A. Hourly
   B. Daily
   C. Weekly
   D. Monthly

    8.____

9. If using a left to right inventory control system, where should new supplies be added?
   A. On the top
   B. In the front
   C. To the left
   D. To the right

    9.____

10. If using a top to bottom inventory control system, where should new supplies be added?
    A. On the top
    B. On the bottom
    C. In the front
    D. In the back

    10.____

11. If using a front to back inventory control system, products should first be distributed from the
    A. front B. back C. right D. left

11.____

12. Which of the following is the only appropriate method to personally transport sterile packs?
    A. Carried in your pocket
    B. Carried under your arm
    C. Carried with hands only
    D. Carried in a paper bag

12.____

13. All transport vehicles, either motorized or manual, should be constructed of materials that allow for proper
    A. delivery
    B. maintenance
    D. decontamination
    D. loading

13.____

14. How often should re-usable covers for carts or other transport vehicles be cleaned?
    A. After each use
    B. After each shift
    C. Daily
    D. Weekly

14.____

15. Dedicated elevators for sterile transport cannot prevent what type of transmission of pathogenic microorganisms?
    A. Food B. Water C. Airborne D. Blood

15.____

16. Due to technology, by what percentage has the need for storage space increased in the 21st century?
    A. 50% B. 100% C. 200% D. 300%

16.____

17. The American Institute of Architects have established guidelines that a facility should have a minimum of _____ ft² space per operating room dedicated for sterile storage.
    A. 25 B. 50 C. 75 D. 100

17.____

18. Which type of system could decrease the amount of instrument space needed for a sterile storage area?
    A. Case cart
    B. Just-in-time
    C. Exchange cart
    D. Requisition

18.____

19. The doors of a sterile supply room should ALWAYS remain
    A. locked B. unlocked C. open D. closed

19.____

20. Sterile supplies should NEVER be stored in which location?
    A. In cabinets B. On shelves C. Under sinks D. On carts

20.____

21. Which agency instituted the guideline that any hospital that chooses to reprocess a single-use device that has been opened and used will be held to the same standards as the original manufacturer of that item?   21.____
    A. Centers for Disease Control and Prevention
    B. Food and Drug Administration
    C. Occupational Health and Safety Administration
    D. National Institute of Health

22. Storage of sterile supplies should be avoided in which of the following locations?   22.____
    A. Windowsills   B. Counters   C. Carts   D. Shelving

23. In the sterile storage area, the temperature is 70°F and the humidity is 69%. What should be done?   23.____
    A. Halt all processes until environment returns to normal
    B. Call maintenance immediately
    C. Continue with routine activities
    D. All instruments in the room must be reprocessed

24. How can damage to medical/surgical supplies stored in the receiving area be avoided?   24.____
    A. Do not distribute until needed
    B. Do not handle excessively
    C. Avoid humidity extremes
    D. Leave supplies in the shipping container

25. The optimum amount of a supply to order is referred to as _____ order quantity.   25.____
    A. economical   B. efficient   C. sustainable   D. usable

KEY (CORRECT ANSWERS)

1. A
2. D
3. B
4. A
5. B

6. A
7. B
8. D
9. D
10. B

11. A
12. C
13. C
14. A
15. C

16. D
17. B
18. A
19. D
20. C

21. D
22. A
23. C
24. C
25. A

EXAMINATION SECTION
TEST 1

DIRECTIONS: Each question or incomplete statement is followed by several suggested answers or completions. Select the one that BEST answers the question or completes the statement. *PRINT THE LETTER OF THE CORRECT ANSWER IN THE SPACE AT THE RIGHT.*

1. Which statement is TRUE when State or local regulations differ from Federal regulations?
   A. The most lenient regulations apply.
   B. The most stringent regulations apply.
   C. State law should always be adhered to.
   D. Federal law should always be adhered to.

   1.____

2. Which agency administers recommendations regarding sterilization procedures?
   A. Association for the Advancement of Medical Instrumentation
   B. American National Standards Institute
   C. Food and Drug Administration
   D. Centers for Disease Control and Prevention

   2.____

3. Healthcare regulations and standards provide consistency of departmental activities by outlining which of the following?
   A. Equal pay practices
   B. Productivity time lines
   C. Employee competency
   D. Minimal performance standards

   3.____

4. Who regulates the established national emissions standards for ethylene oxide used by hospitals?
   A. National Institute of Health
   B. Environmental Protection Agency
   C. Occupational Safety and Health Administration
   D. There are no established national emissions standards

   4.____

5. Standards and regulations help set levels of all of the following in medical departments EXCEPT
   A. quality   B. safety   C. competency   D. efficiency

   5.____

6. Which agency may intervene in a matter of worker protections even if there are no specific regulations covering the situation?
   A. Department of Labor
   B. Occupational Safety and Health Administration
   C. Environmental Protection Agency
   D. Association of PeriOperative Registered Nurses

   6.____

7. Which agency imposes very strict labeling requirements on manufacturers of chemicals used by Central Service Departments?
    A. Food and Drug Administration
    B. Centers for Disease Control and Prevention
    C. Environmental Protection Agency
    D. Occupational Safety and Health Administration

8. Which agency is responsible for regulating third party processors?
    A. Environmental Protection Agency
    B. Association for the Advancement of Medical Instrumentation
    C. American National Standards Institute
    D. Food and Drug Administration

9. Failure to receive accreditation from which of the following agencies can result in the loss of Medicare and Medicaid reimbursements?
    A. Joint Commission
    B. Centers for Disease Control and Prevention
    C. Environmental Protection Agency
    D. Occupational Safety and Health Administration

10. Historically, what department was responsible for the majority of the employee-related record keeping?
    A. Medical staff
    B. Human Resources
    C. Employee health
    D. Hospital administration

11. Which organization does NOT seek proof that all Central Service employees have been properly trained and are competent in their job?
    A. Joint Commission
    B. Centers for Medicare and Medicaid Services
    C. Occupational Safety and Health Administration
    D. Department of Environmental Protection

12. Every Central Service employee should have ongoing training and competency assessed in all of the following areas EXCEPT
    A. equipment troubleshooting
    B. decontamination
    C. distribution processes
    D. tray assembly

13. Safety training should be documented for Central Service employees in all of the following areas EXCEPT
    A. hazardous chemicals used in the Department
    B. use of material safety data sheets
    C. facility's hazard communication program
    D. use of radiation within the Department

14. Training records must contain all of the following EXCEPT
    A. location of training
    B. date of training
    C. results of competency testing
    D. signature of person observing competency testing

15. Which agency requires records of employee injuries such as needle sticks, sharps incidents, and ethylene oxide exposure?
    A. Department of Labor
    B. Centers for Disease Control and Prevention
    C. Occupational Safety and Health Administration
    D. Food and Drug Administration

    15.____

16. How often must workplace injuries be maintained in a log and reported to OSHA?
    A. Weekly
    B. Monthly
    C. Every 6 months
    D. Annually

    16.____

17. Who is responsible for providing maintenance for steam sterilizers?
    A. Central Service Director
    B. Central Service Employees
    C. Qualified Service Technician
    D. Sterilizer Manufacturer

    17.____

18. How long should documentation regarding sterilizer service be retained?
    A. 2 years
    B. 5 years
    C. 7 years
    D. For the life of the equipment

    18.____

19. Which of the following does NOT need to be included in maintenance and repair records for sterilizers?
    A. Type of repairs
    B. Part utilized
    C. Cost of repairs
    D. Verification testing

    19.____

20. All of the following should be reviewed periodically to determine if there are repairs or trends that require further analysis?
    A. Positive biological indicators
    B. Positive biological indicators
    C. Wet packs
    D. Sterilizer process failures

    20.____

21. What test must be performed immediately after steam sterilizer installation or a major repair?
    A. Biological indicator
    B. Bowie-Dick Test
    C. Chemical Indicator
    D. Toxicological Indicator

    21.____

22. A biological indicator is required for each sterilization cycle that contains which type of items?
    A. Powered instruments
    B. Sharp instruments
    C. Endoscopes
    D. Implantable items

    22.____

23. Which test should be run and documented at least daily before the first process load and after any dynamic air removal sterilizer shutdown or repair?
    A. Biological indicator
    B. Bowie-Dick Test
    C. Chemical indicator
    D. Toxicological indicator

    23.____

4 (#1)

24. What should be documented and retained with all sterilizer load information that will allow facility personnel to trace a sterilized package to the exact date and processing time, as well as sterilizer load contents if there is a need for a recall? 24.____
    A. Chemical indicators
    B. Instrument serial numbers
    C. Lot control number
    D. Biological indicators

25. Which of the following should be maintained in order to document every item sterilized in each sterilizer load and contain the sterilizer cycle parameters specific to the documented cycle? 25.____
    A. Load log
    B. Lot control number
    C. Inventory log
    D. Department process log

KEY (CORRECT ANSWERS)

1.	B		11.	D
2.	A		12.	A
3.	D		13.	D
4.	D		14.	A
5.	C		15.	C
6.	B		16.	D
7.	C		17.	C
8.	D		18.	D
9.	A		19.	C
10.	B		20.	B

21. A
22. D
23. B
24. C
25. A

TEST 2

DIRECTIONS: Each question or incomplete statement is followed by several suggested answers or completions. Select the one that BEST answers the question or completes the statement. *PRINT THE LETTER OF THE CORRECT ANSWER IN THE SPACE AT THE RIGHT.*

1. At the minimum, all of the following parameters should be documented for every sterilizer cycle that is run EXCEPT
    A. Sterilizer temperature
    B. Room temperature
    C. Cycle time
    D. Name of Central Service Technician running the cycle

    1.____

2. Flash sterilizer documentation should be traceable to the exact
    A. instrument that was used
    B. operating room in which it was used
    C. patient on which the item was used
    D. procedure for which the item was used

    2.____

3. For low temperature sterilization processes, how often must biological indicators be run and documented?
    A. In every low temperature cycle
    B. Hourly
    C. Daily
    D. Weekly

    3.____

4. Ethylene oxide requires more documentation than other types of low temperature stabilizers because ethylene oxide is
    A. flammable
    B. corrosive
    C. classified as a mutagen
    D. reactive with water

    4.____

5. Although there are no standards regulating ethylene oxide sterilization in every state, which agency requires that exposure levels in work areas breathing zones be carefully monitored?
    A. Department of Labor
    B. Environmental Protection Agency
    C. Occupational Safety and Health Administration
    D. Food and Drug Administration

    5.____

6. To ensure compliance, ethylene oxide sterilization zones should have air sampling values that are regulated to _____ ppm levels.
    A. 1   B. 2   C. 3   D. 5

    6.____

7. In addition to the regulated levels, the action levels for ethylene oxide zones should be less than _____ ppm levels.
    A. 0.2   B. 0.5   C. 0.8   D. 1.0

    7.____

8. How often should air sampling testing be performed within areas of ethylene oxide sterilization?
   A. Weekly   B. Monthly   C. Twice yearly   D. Yearly

   8._____

9. Which of the following does NOT need to be included in the air sampling documentation for ethylene oxide sterilizers?
   A. Ethylene oxide concentration levels
   B. Proof the sampling results were shared with employees
   C. Name and Social Security numbers of monitored employees
   D. Serial number of equipment used for sampling

   9._____

10. If an actual ethylene oxide exposure has occurred, how long must the documents be retained after the affected employee's last day of employment?
    A. 1 year   B. 5 years   C. 10 years   D. 30 years

    10._____

11. High-level disinfection has become more common in recent years for the processing of _____ items.
    A. disposable   B. implantable   C. semi-critical   D. critical

    11._____

12. How often do most manufacturers recommend testing of glutaraldehyde and ortho-phthalaldelyde disinfectant solutions?
    A. Prior to each use   B. Hourly
    C. Daily   D. Weekly

    12._____

13. What information needs does NOT need to be documented when testing high-level disinfectant solutions?
    A. Date disinfectant was acquired
    B. Expiration date of the disinfectant
    C. Expiration date of test strip
    D. Person conducting the test

    13._____

14. When testing glutaraldehyde solutions, the level of glutaraldehyde must exceed the _____ level.
    A. 1%   B. 2%   C. 3%   D. 4%

    14._____

15. When testing ortho-phthalaldelyde solutions, the level of ortho-phthalaldelyde must exceed the _____ level.
    A. 1%   B. 2%   C. 3%   D. 4%

    15._____

16. Which two agencies recommend routine monitoring of the temperature of water-decontaminators?
    A. AAMI/ANSI   B. FDA/EPA   C. SGNA/CDC   D. OSHA/FDA

    16._____

17. In addition to water temperature, what is also recommended to be monitored and documented regarding water-decontaminators?
    A. Water pH level   B. Cleaning ability
    C. Number of uses   D. Length of cycle

    17._____

18. Documentation of water-decontaminators should include all of the following EXCEPT the
    A. type of test used
    B. date of the test
    C. person performing test
    D. load information

19. With the exception of ethylene oxide exposure documentation, who sets the standards for retaining records for the Central Service Department?
    A. Food and Drug Administration
    B. Centers for Disease Control and Prevention
    C. Occupational Safety and Health Administration
    D. Individual Facility Risk Management and Legal Departments

20. Most facilities maintain their sterilizer records for _____ year(s).
    A. 1   B. 2   C. 3   D. 5

21. Most facilities that treat newborn babies maintain their records for _____ years.
    A. 5   B. 10   C. 17   D. 21

22. All of the following may be documented using electronic instrument tracking EXCEPT _____ records.
    A. tray processing
    B. sterilization
    C. biological
    D. air sampling

23. In what location should a lot control number be affixed?
    A. On the sterilizer
    B. On each instrument
    C. On each instrument pack
    D. On the patient's medical record

24. What type of sterilizer does not require the use of lot control numbers?
    A. Flash sterilizer
    B. Steam sterilizer
    C. Ethylene oxide sterilizer
    D. water decontaminators

25. Which statement is TRUE regarding documentation of actual ethylene oxide exposures?
    Documentation must
    A. contain written opinions of any physicians.
    B. include a plan to return exposure concentrations below the action level
    C. include every person who enters the Central Service Department until the action level has been restored
    D. be retained for at least 30 years after the affected employee's last day of employment

KEY (CORRECT ANSWERS)

1.	B	11.	C
2.	C	12.	A
3.	A	13.	A
4.	C	14.	B
5.	C	15.	C
6.	A	16.	A
7.	B	17.	B
8.	C	18.	D
9.	D	19.	D
10.	D	20.	C

21. D
22. D
23. C
24. A
25. C

TEST 3

DIRECTIONS: Each question or incomplete statement is followed by several suggested answers or completions. Select the one that BEST answers the question or completes the statement. *PRINT THE LETTER OF THE CORRECT ANSWER IN THE SPACE AT THE RIGHT.*

1. Which of the following incidents is NOT qualified to be reported to the Occupational Safety and Health Administration?
    A. A nurse being stuck with a needle
    B. Off-duty hospital employee falls in the hospital while visiting a family member
    C. Central Service employee is directly exposed to ethylene oxide
    D. Central service employee getting burned from faulty power equipment

1.____

2. Once an incident has been deemed appropriate to report to OSHA, how long do you have to fill out the necessary paperwork?
    A. Within 24 hours
    B. Within 48 hours
    C. Within 7 days
    D. Within 30 days

2.____

3. What is the time frame required to report any work-related death to OSHA?
    A. Within 8 hours
    B. Within 12 hours
    C. Within 24 hours
    D. Within 48 hours

3.____

4. Under current regulations, which of the following is NOT required to report suspected medical device deaths to the Food and Drug Administration?
    A. Device manufacturer
    B. Hospitals
    C. Hospital employees
    D. Outpatient clinics

4.____

5. Which organization is responsible for initiating and advancing international cooperation for the improvement of health conditions?
    A. Centers for Disease Control and Prevention
    B. World Health Organization
    C. National Institute of Health
    D. Food and Drug Administration

5.____

6. Which organization is responsible for developing nationally recognized standards, recommend practices, and guidelines for the Peri-Operative setting?
    A. Occupational Safety and Health Administration
    B. Food and Drug Administration
    C. Association of PeriOperative Registered Nurses
    D. American Nurses Association

6.____

7. Which of the following organizations enhances global competitiveness and quality of life by promoting standards and insuring their integrity?
    A. Occupational Safety and Health Administration
    B. Environmental Protection Agency
    C. Society for Gastroenterology Nurses and Associates
    D. American National Standards Institute

7.____

8. Which of the following organizations provide standards and evaluations for healthcare facilities and perform on on-site inspection every three years?
    A. Centers for Disease Control and Prevention
    B. World Health Organization
    C. Environmental Protection Agency
    D. Joint Commission

9. Which organization is a voluntary international organization that is dedicated to the prevention and control of infections and related outcomes?
    A. World Health Organization
    B. Centers for Disease Control and Prevention
    C. Association for Professionals in Infection Control
    D. National Institute of Health

10. Which organization is responsible for creating and revising standards for processing water for irrigation?
    A. United States Pharmacopoeia-National Formulary
    B. Centers for Disease Control and Prevention
    C. Food and Drug Administration
    D. Environmental Protection Agency

11. Which organization is responsible for enforcing laws in regards to the transportation of medical wastes?
    A. Department of Transportation
    B. Environmental Protection Agency
    C. Food and Drug Administration
    D. Centers for Disease Control and Prevention

12. Which organization is considered to be the GREATEST resource for healthcare guidelines?
    A. Food and Drug Administration
    B. Centers for Disease Control and Prevention
    C. Association for the Advancement of Medical Instruments
    D. American National Standards Institute

13. The responsibility of which agency is to set and enforce international standards to reduce the burden of fire and other hazards?
    A. American National Standards Institute
    B. Environmental Protection Agency
    C. National Fire Protection Agency
    D. National Institute of Health

14. Which agency is responsible for promoting health by preventing and controlling disease?
    A. World Health Organization
    B. Association for Professionals in Infection Control
    C. Centers for Disease Control and Prevention
    D. National Institute of Health

15. Which agency is responsible for the MedWatch program?
    A. Food and Drug Administration
    B. Centers for Disease Control and Prevention
    C. World Health Organization
    D. Environmental Protection Agency

16. The guidelines of which agency are considered to be voluntary?
    A. Environmental Protection Agency
    B. Department of Transportation
    C. Association for the Advancement of Medical Instruments
    D. Food and Drug Administration

17. The guidelines of which agency are considered to be regulatory?
    A. Occupational Safety and Health Administration
    B. American National Standards Institute
    C. Centers for Disease Control and Prevention
    D. Joint Commission

18. Which agency sets the standards to prevent against blood-borne pathogens?
    A. Food and Drug Administration
    B. Centers for Disease Control and Prevention
    C. Occupational Safety and Health Administration
    D. World Health Organization

19. Which of the following is NOT considered to be a blood-borne pathogen?
    A. HIV   B. Hepatitis A   C. Hepatitis B   D. Hepatitis C

20. Employers must make what type of vaccination available to all workers with potential occupational exposure?
    A. Hepatitis B   B. Hepatitis C   C. Influenza   D. Pneumonia

21. A blood-borne pathogen exposure incident does NOT include which of the following body parts?
    A. Eyes   B. Mouth   C. Intact skin   D. Non-intact skin

22. What color should containers carrying potential blood-borne pathogens be?
    A. Yellow   B. Red   C. Black   D. Blue

23. How often must employers provide training in regards to blood-borne pathogens?
    A. Weekly
    B. Monthly
    C. Twice annually
    D. Annually

24. The Occupational Safety and Health Administration requires that all work-related in-patient hospitalizations, amputations, and losses of any eye are within _____ hours.
    A. 8   B. 12   C. 24   D. 48

25. What percentage of blood-borne pathogen exposures can be prevented 25.____
through the use of personal protective equipment?
    A. 50%   B. 65%   C. 77%   D. 88%

KEY (CORRECT ANSWERS)

1.	B	11.	A
2.	C	12.	C
3.	A	13.	C
4.	C	14.	C
5.	B	15.	A
6.	C	16.	C
7.	D	17.	A
8.	D	18.	C
9.	C	19.	B
10.	A	20.	A

21. C
22. B
23. D
24. C
25. D

TEST 4

DIRECTIONS: Each question or incomplete statement is followed by several suggested answers or completions. Select the one that BEST answers the question or completes the statement. *PRINT THE LETTER OF THE CORRECT ANSWER IN THE SPACE AT THE RIGHT.*

1. In what year was the Needlestick Safety and Prevention Act signed into law? 1.____
   A. 1991 B. 1996 C. 2000 D. 2003

2. What information is NOT required to be documented in a sharps injury log? 2.____
   A. Type and brand of device
   B. Bodily location of injury
   C. Where incident occurred
   D. Explanation of how injury occurred

3. How often should a facility's written blood-borne pathogens exposure control plan be reviewed and updated? 3.____
   A. Monthly
   B. Quarterly
   C. Twice annually
   D. Annually

4. Which of the following is NOT accepted by OSHA as an appropriate disinfectant to prevent against the spread of HIV and Hepatitis B? 4.____
   A. Soap and water
   B. Tuberculocidal disinfectants
   C. Diluted bleach solutions
   D. Properly labeled EPA-registered disinfectants

5. After completion of the three-dose Hepatitis B vaccination, what time period should elapse before a worker be tested for immunity against Hepatitis B? 5.____
   A. 7 days B. 30 days C. 60-90 days D. 120 days

6. What is the proper procedure if a worker is not immune to Hepatitis B after the three-dose vaccination? 6.____
   A. Document as such and allow the person to work
   B. Repeat the vaccination series and retest
   C. Do not permit the employee to work until immunity has been established
   D. No actions needs to be taken

7. Which agency set the guidelines that OSHA adheres to in regards to Hepatitis B? 7.____
   A. World Health Organization
   B. United States Public Health Service
   C. American Medical Association
   D. Centers for Disease Control and Prevention

8. When decontaminating an area that is potentially contaminated with the HIV virus, the surface must be left wet with the disinfectant for _____ seconds. 8.____
   A. 30 B. 60 C. 120 D. 300

9. When decontaminating an area that is potentially contaminated with the Hepatitis B virus, the surface must be left wet with the disinfectant for _____ minute(s).
   A. 1   B. 3   C. 6   D. 10

10. Which of the following is NOT necessary to be included for training of individuals regarding methods to prevent or reduce exposure to blood-borne pathogens?
    A. Appropriate engineering controls
    B. Characteristics of blood
    C. Work practices
    D. Personal protective equipment

11. The sharps injury log must be recorded and maintained in a manner that protects the _____ of the injured worker.
    A. confidentiality   B. integrity   C. reputation   D. competency

12. Which of the following is OSHA mandated to be work to protect workers against exposure to blood-borne pathogens?
    A. Respirators
    B. Personal protective equipment
    C. Scrubs
    D. Lead aprons

13. The FDA's policy on labeling of liquid chemical sterilants and high-level disinfectants does not require references to which of the following?
    A. Safe and effective use of the product
    B. List of active ingredients
    C. Concentration of active ingredients
    D. Specific diseases

14. Users should be able to infer the _____ efficacy of a product by examining the FDA-cleared claims for use in sterilization or high-level disinfection.
    A. tuberculocidal   B. microbiocidal
    C. viricidal   D. fungicidal

15. The _____ program is mandatory for death/permanent disability events and also encourages voluntary reporting of any device related problems or adverse events?
    A. MarketWatch   B. MedWatch
    C. Sentinel Event   D. MedRecall

16. Which agency is responsible for regulating the re-use of single-use devices?
    A. Association for the Advancement of Medical Instruments
    B. Occupational Safety and Health Administration
    C. Food and Drug Administration
    D. Centers for Disease Control and Prevention

17. Under which piece of legislation does the Environmental Protection Agency regulate the use of ethylene oxide?   17.____
    A. Federal Safe Medical Standards Act
    B. Federal Insecticide, Fungicide, and Rodenticide Act
    C. Federal Safe Medical Practices Act
    D. Federal Medical Device Act

18. As of January 1, 2015, which product was phased out and discontinued for use in Central Service Departments by the Environmental Protection Agency?   18.____
    A. Ozone   B. Oxyfume
    C. Ethylene oxide   D. Hydrogen peroxide

19. According to the Environmental Protection Agency, a disinfectant is considered to be misused in all of the following cases EXCEPT when the   19.____
    A. product is diluted
    B. contact time of the product is altered
    C. recommended method of application is not followed
    D. recommended method of absorption is not followed

20. The Association of Advancement of Medical Instruments develops standards and recommended practices based on which of the following?   20.____
    A. Good practices   B. Revenue enhancements
    C. Licensure regulations   D. Surgical procedures

21. What is the purpose of an MSDS sheet?   21.____
    A. Provide operating instructions for medical devices
    B. Provide cleaning instructions for medical devices
    C. Provide assembly instructions for endoscopes
    D. Provide information about chemicals used by employees

22. The Occupational Safety and Health Administration has established occupational exposure limits for which of the following?   22.____
    A. Sterilization temperatures   B. Sterile storage temperatures
    C. Sterilants and disinfection   D. Radiation

23. If the Environmental Protection Agency deems a product safe for use, what are the product and associated labeling given before it can be sold?   23.____
    A. Sales tax code   B. License with approval code
    C. EPA registration number   D. Unique product identifier

24. Which of the following is NOT a document supported by the Association for the Advancement of Medical Instruments as a guideline for Central Service employees?
    A. Surgical patient volume fluctuations based on standard and planned reimbursements
    B. Comprehensive guide to steam sterilization and sterility assurance in healthcare facilities
    C. Chemical sterilization and high-level disinfection in healthcare facilities
    D. Ethylene oxide sterilization in healthcare facilities: safety and effectiveness

25. Which of the following is contained in the Peri-Operative Standards and Recommended Practices?
    A. AORN guidelines for manufacturing surgical instruments
    B. Nursing staffing patterns for normal surgical procedures in the United States
    C. AORN expense practices for allocating patient costs between facility departments
    D. AORN approved standards, guidelines, recommended practices, and guidance statements

KEY (CORRECT ANSWERS)

1.	C	11.	A
2.	B	12.	B
3.	D	13.	D
4.	A	14.	B
5.	C	15.	B
6.	B	16.	D
7.	B	17.	B
8.	A	18.	B
9.	D	19.	D
10.	B	20.	A

21.	D
22.	C
23.	C
24.	A
25.	D

EXAMINATION SECTION
TEST 1

DIRECTIONS: Each question or incomplete statement is followed by several suggested answers or completions. Select the one that BEST answers the question or completes the statement. *PRINT THE LETTER OF THE CORRECT ANSWER IN THE SPACE AT THE RIGHT.*

1. Which of the following is NOT considered to be a safe practice? 1.____
   A. Discard open sterile bottles.
   B. Sterile persons drape first toward themselves, then away.
   C. Sterile persons face sterile areas
   D. Sterile tables may be covered for future use.

2. What is the MINIMUM distance a nonsterile person should remain from a sterile field? 2.____
   A. 1 foot   B. 3 feet   C. 5 feet   D. 10 feet

3. Which of the following is NOT an acceptable wrapper for gas sterilization? 3.____
   A. Nylon   B. Muslin   C. Paper   D. Plastic

4. Which of the following is the only acceptable plastic that can be used for a steam sterilization wrapper? 4.____
   A. Polyethylene   B. Polypropylene
   C. Polyamide   D. Polyvinyl chloride

5. All of the following statements are true regarding muslin wrappers EXCEPT: 5.____
   A. Muslin must be laundered, even if unused, in order to rehydrate it.
   B. A 140 thread count of unbleached muslin is used for wrappers.
   C. Muslin is flexible and easy to handle.
   D. Small holes can be repaired by stitching on a patch.

6. _____ days is the MAXIMUM storage life for a muslin wrapped item in a closed cabinet. 6.____
   A. 7   B. 14   C. 21   D. 30

7. Which of the following statements is FALSE regarding the scrub procedure? 7.____
   A. It reduces microbial count.   B. It leaves an antimicrobial residue.
   C. It renders the skin aseptic.   D. It removes skin oil.

8. Which statement regarding removal of gown and gloves FAILS to meet safe criteria? 8.____
   A. Gloves are removed before the gown.
   B. The gown is pulled off inside out.
   C. The scrub nurse pulls the gloves off.
   D. The scrub uses closed-glove technique to reapply gloves.

9. Which of the following statements regarding the surgical scrub is NOT an acceptable practice?
   A. Fingernails should not extend beyond the tip of the finger.
   B. Nail polish may be worn if it is freshly applied.
   C. Staff members with cuts, abrasions, or hangnails should not scrub in.
   D. A non-oil-based hand lotion may be used to protect the skin.

10. How many pounds of pressure is required of a steam sterilizer set at 250°F?
    A. 8-10   B. 11-14   C. 15-17   D. 18-21

11. The MINIMUM exposure time for unwrapped instruments in a flash sterilizer that is set at 270°F is _____ minutes.
    A. 3   B. 5   C. 7   D. 10

12. To be sterilized effectively, a linen pack must not weigh more than _____ lbs.
    A. 5   B. 8   C. 12   D. 15

13. All of the following statements are true regarding instrument sets EXCEPT:
    A. Instruments must be placed in perforated trays.
    B. Heavy instruments are placed on the bottom
    C. All instruments must be closed.
    D. All detachable parts must be disassembled.

14. All of the following statements are true regarding steam sterilization EXCEPT:
    A. Flat packages are placed on the shelf.
    B. Small packages placed one on top of the other are criss-crossed.
    C. Basins are placed on their sides.
    D. Solutions may be autoclaved along with other items as long as they are on a shelf alone.

15. Wrapped basin sets must be sterilized by steam under a pressure of 250°F for a MINIMUM of _____ minutes.
    A. 10   B. 20   C. 30   D. 40

16. Which of the following statements is TRUE regarding the sterilization of basin sets?
    A. Basins must be separated by a porous material if they are nested.
    B. Sponges and linen may be packaged inside the basin to be sterilized.
    C. Basins are placed flat in the autoclave.
    D. Basins must always be placed on the top shelf of the autoclave in a combined load.

17. Which of the following is critical when using activated glutaraldehyde for sterilization?
    A. Items must be rinsed thoroughly in sterile water prior to use.
    B. Solution must be heated in order to be effective.
    C. Items must be thoroughly moistened prior to placement in the solution.
    D. Items must be air dried prior to use.

18. The shelf life of glutaraldehyde if _____ days. 18._____
    A. 7-10   B. 10-14   C. 20-24   D. 24-28

19. In order to kill spores, an item must be immersed in a 2% aqueous solution 19._____
    of glutaraldehyde for _____ hours.
    A. 2   B. 6   C. 10   D. 12

20. _____ is a process in which air bubbles are imploded and burst inward 20._____
    causing the release of particles of soil or tissue debris.
    A. Sterilization   B. Cavitation
    C. Autoclaving   D. Decontamination

21. Which high level disinfectant is effective on surfaces, floors, and equipment? 21._____
    A. Sodium hypochlorite
    B. Alcohol
    C. Carbolic acid
    D. Quaternary ammonium compounds

22. Sodium hypochlorite forms a highly carcinogenic solution if it becomes mixed 22._____
    with
    A. alcohol   B. betadine
    C. formaldehyde   D. acetone

23. Which intermediate level disinfectant is a highly concentrated solution 23._____
    that can be easily diluted?
    A. Glutaraldehyde   B. Sodium hypochlorite
    C. Alcohol   D. Carbolic acid

24. Which intermediate level disinfectant is low cost, easy to mix with water, 24._____
    odorless, and non-corrosive on metals?
    A. Sodium hypochlorite
    B. Alcohol
    C. Carolic acid
    D. Quaternary ammonium compounds

25. Which intermediate level disinfectant is non-sporicidal, highly flammable, 25._____
    and effective against many microbes including HIV?
    A. Sodium hypochlorite
    B. Alcohol
    C. Carbolic acid
    D. Quaternary ammonium compounds

KEY (CORRECT ANSWERS)

1.	D	11.	A
2.	A	12.	C
3.	A	13.	C
4.	B	14.	D
5.	D	15.	B
6.	D	16.	A
7.	C	17.	A
8.	A	18.	D
9.	B	19.	C
10.	C	20.	B

21. A
22. C
23. D
24. D
25. D

TEST 2

DIRECTIONS: Each question or incomplete statement is followed by several suggested answers or completions. Select the one that BEST answers the question or completes the statement. *PRINT THE LETTER OF THE CORRECT ANSWER IN THE SPACE AT THE RIGHT.*

1. Which presoaking solution keeps organic debris moist?
   A. Enzymes B. Sterile water
   C. Alcohol D. Detergent
   1.____

2. Which presoaking solution removes moistened and dried debris without the need for mechanical action?
   A. Enzymes B. Sterile water
   C. Alcohol D. Detergent
   2.____

3. _____ is a surface acting agent that lowers the surface tension of a liquid so it can penetrate deeper and prevents debris from being re-deposited on the item to which the soil was attached.
   A. Lipase B. Amylase
   C. Surfactant D. Hydrogen peroxide
   3.____

4. Bath temperatures over _____°F will coagulate protein and make it more difficult to remove.
   A. 80 B. 100 C. 120 D. 140
   4.____

5. What is the PROPER bath temperature for cleaning instruments?
   A. 70-99°F B. 80-109°F C. 90-119°F D. 100-129°F
   5.____

6. _____ refers to the removal of any residue of cleaning agents and chemical remaining after the cleaning process and is necessary regardless of whether a manual or mechanical cleaning process was used.
   A. Impingement B. Free rinsing
   C. Decontaminating D. Disinfecting
   6.____

7. _____ are chemicals that hold hard water minerals in solution and prevent soaps or detergents from reacting with the minerals.
   A. Protease enzymes B. Chelating agents
   C. Sequestering agents D. Detergents
   7.____

8. _____ are chemicals that remove or inactive hard water minerals.
   A. Protease enzymes B. Chelating agents
   C. Sequestering agents D. Detergents
   8.____

9. Which type of wrapping is made of cotton or blends of cotton/polyester and must be inspected for lint, holes, worn areas, and stains?
   A. Woven textiles
   B. Woven textiles with barrier properties
   C. Non-woven materials
   D. Rigid instrument containers

9.____

10. Which type of wrapping is made of cotton/polyester blend, chemical treated for moisture resistances, and requires two wrappers per instrument set?
    A. Woven textiles
    B. Woven textiles with barrier properties
    C. Non-woven materials
    D. Rigid instrument containers

10.____

11. Which type of steam sterilizer tests for air removal daily with a Bowie-Dick test?
    A. Flash sterilization
    B. Autoclave
    C. Gravity displacement
    D. Pre-vacuum steam sterilizer

11.____

12. Which type of sterilization method uses radio frequency waves at a low temperature, is a dry process, sterilization occurs in one hour, and forms radicals that interact with the cell membrane which kills the microbes?
    A. Ozone gas sterilizer
    B. Chlorine dioxide gas
    C. Plasma sterilization
    D. Vapor phase hydrogen peroxide

12.____

13. Which type of sterilization oxidizes bacteria, is destructive to rubber and plastics, corrosive for some metals, and should not be used on long-cannulated instruments?
    A. Ozone gas sterilizer
    B. Chlorine dioxide gas
    C. Plasma sterilization
    D. Vapor phase hydrogen peroxide

13.____

14. The preparation and packaging must have an air exchange rate of _____ per hour.
    A. 4   B. 6   C. 8   D. 10

14.____

15. What is the acceptable temperature range for the preparation and packaging area?
    A. 60-65°F   B. 70-75°F   C. 75-80°F   D. 80-85°F

15.____

16. Which of the following represents the ideal humidity level in the preparation and packaging area?
    A. 20%   B. 35%   C. 40%   D. 50%

16.____

17. Which of the following statements is TRUE when a non-perforated tray is used for the sterilization of instrument sets?
    A. Must be wrapped with a towel prior to instrument placement
    B. Must be processed on the top rack of the sterilizer
    C. Must be laid flat on the sterilizer rack
    D. Must be tilted on the sterilizer rack

17.____

18. Which of the following statements is TRUE regarding the floors of the preparation area?   18._____
    A. Should be wet-mopped daily
    B. Should be dry-mopped each shift
    C. Should be vacuumed once per week
    D. Should be broom-swept hourly

19. When assembling an instrument set containing heavy and delicate objects, where should the heavier instruments be placed?   19._____
    A. On top of the delicate instruments
    B. On the bottom of the set
    C. In the center of the tray
    D. On the right-hand side

20. Which of the following can be performed to assist in the drying of wrapped instrument sets?   20._____
    A. Place the set on a transfer tray.
    B. Place instruments in foam dividers.
    C. Place a towel in the bottom of the tray.
    D. Place silicone mats in the bottom of the tray.

21. In what location should the chemical indicator be placed in a wrapped set of instruments?   21._____
    A. In the left-hand corner   B. In the center of the set
    C. In two opposing corners   D. On the right-hand side

22. Where should chemical indicators be placed for multi-layer container systems?   22._____
    A. In the middle of the tray   B. In the bottom level
    C. On each level   D. In each corner

23. What is the MAXIMUM size and weight of a textile pack?   23._____
    A. 10"x12"x12" / 20 lbs.   B. 12"x20"x10" / 7.2 lbs.
    C. 12"x12"x12" / 10 lbs.   D. 12"x12"x20" / 12 lbs.

24. Which of the following statements is TRUE regarding preparation of basin sets for sterilization?   24._____
    A. Basins should be separated by at least ½ inch.
    B. Basins should be placed in opposing directions.
    C. An absorbent material should be placed between each basin.
    D. A non-absorbent material should be placed between each basin.

25. All of the following are basic principles of packaging EXCEPT: 25._____
    A. A package must be able to be opened without contamination.
    B. Packing material must be acceptable for all types of sterilization.
    C. Packing material must allow the sterilant to reach the contents.
    D. The packing material must be a barrier to microorganisms.

KEY (CORRECT ANSWERS)

1. B
2. B
3. C
4. D
5. B

6. B
7. B
8. C
9. A
10. A

11. D
12. C
13. A
14. A
15. B

16. C
17. D
18. A
19. D
20. C

21. B
22. C
23. D
24. C
25. B

TEST 3

DIRECTIONS: Each question or incomplete statement is followed by several suggested answers or completions. Select the one that BEST answers the question or completes the statement. *PRINT THE LETTER OF THE CORRECT ANSWER IN THE SPACE AT THE RIGHT.*

1. Which of the following can inhibit the penetration of sterilant? 1.____
   A. A wrapper that is too small
   B. A wrapper that is too large
   C. An envelope fold on a small set
   D. A square fold on a large deck

2. Approximately how much space should be left between an item and the inside edges of a peel pouch? 2.____
   A. 1 inch   B. 2 inches   C. 3 inches   D. 4 inches

3. Which of the following packaging materials is acceptable for steam sterilization? 3.____
   A. Tyvek
   B. Polyethylene
   C. Aluminum foil
   D. Non-woven wraps

4. Which of the following packaging materials is acceptable for low-temperature glass plasma sterilization? 4.____
   A. Paper pouches
   B. Polyethylene
   C. Aluminum foil
   D. Non-woven wraps

5. Tamper-evident seals on rigid containers include 5.____
   A. lids and gaskets
   B. lids and latches
   C. latches and locks
   D. filters and gaskets

6. During the sterilization process, rigid containers must be placed 6.____
   A. flat
   B. on their side
   C. on the top shelf
   D. on the middle shelf

7. What series of stainless steel is used to manufacturer malleable retractors? 7.____
   A. 200   B. 300   C. 400   D. 500

8. Which of the following would be used to hold back the intestines during an abdominal procedure? 8.____
   A. Kelly clamp
   B. Deaver retractor
   C. Debakey forcep
   D. Greenberg retractor

9. What is the MOST difficult part of a hemostat to clean? 9.____
   A. Box lock   B. Ratchet   C. Shanks   D. Jaws

10. What is the FINAL stage in the process of manufacturing of a surgical grade instrument? 10.____
    A. Cavitation
    B. Lubrication
    C. Passivation
    D. Ebonization

101

11. Scissors with black handles are often referred to as
    A. satin
    B. martensitic
    C. super sharps
    D. surgical grade

12. The layer on a surgical instrument created by the passivation process is called
    A. satin finish
    B. tungsten carbide
    C. chromium oxide
    D. an ebonized surface

13. What is the EASIEST method to identify an instrument with tungsten carbide inserts?
    A. Black handles
    B. Gold handles
    C. Satin finish
    D. Shiny finish

14. What type of finish is on a surgical instrument that is used for laser procedures?
    A. Gold
    B. Satin
    C. Shiny
    D. Ebonized

15. Unless otherwise directed by the manufacturer, how often should an instrument be lubricated?
    A. After every use
    B. Daily
    C. Weekly
    D. Monthly

16. The air flow in the preparation and packaging area must be maintained at _____ pressure.
    A. positive
    B. negative
    C. constant
    D. automatic

17. For what time period should service records on sterilizer equipment be maintained?
    A. 1 year
    B. 3 years
    C. 5 years
    D. For the life of the equipment

18. A biological indicator is required with each sterilization cycle containing
    A. disposable items
    B. sharps
    C. heavy equipment
    D. implantable devices

19. How often do dynamic air removal sterilizers require the use of a Bowie-Dick test?
    A. After every load
    B. Daily
    C. Weekly
    D. Monthly

20. With what type of sterilization should the documentation be tracked directly to the patient for which the item was used?
    A. Flash sterilization
    B. Autoclave
    C. Gravity displacement
    D. Pre-vacuum steam sterilizer

21. If an employee has had an ethylene oxide exposure, records must be maintained _____ after employee's last day of employment.
    A. 30 days
    B. 6 months
    C. 10 years
    D. 30 years

3 (#3)

22. Most manufacturers recommend testing high-level disinfectant solutions how often? 22.____
    A. Prior to each use   B. Daily
    C. Weekly   D. Monthly

23. Records are kept for facilities who treat newborn babies for a time period of _____ years. 23.____
    A. 7   B. 10   C. 18   D. 21

24. Ethylene oxide sterilizers require more documentation than other types of low temperature sterilizers because ethylene oxide has been classified as a 24.____
    A. antigen   B. pathogen   C. carcinogen   D. histogen

25. Which of the following must be affixed to each package that is sterilized to allow facility personnel to trace a sterilized package to the exact date and processing time, sterilizer, and load contents if there is a need for a recall? 25.____
    A. Biological indicator   B. Chemical indicator
    C. Lot control number   D. Load log

KEY (CORRECT ANSWERS)

1.	B	11.	C
2.	A	12.	C
3.	D	13.	B
4.	D	14.	D
5.	C	15.	A
6.	A	16.	A
7.	B	17.	D
8.	B	18.	D
9.	A	19.	B
10.	C	20.	A

21.	D
22.	A
23.	D
24.	C
25.	C

TEST 4

DIRECTIONS: Each question or incomplete statement is followed by several suggested answers or completions. Select the one that BEST answers the question or completes the statement. *PRINT THE LETTER OF THE CORRECT ANSWER IN THE SPACE AT THE RIGHT.*

1. If an incident requires a report be sent to OSHA, the necessary paperwork must be submitted within a time period of _____ days. 1._____
    A. 8   B. 10   C. 14   D. 30

2. A work related death must be reported to OSHA within a time frame of _____ hours. 2._____
    A. 4   B. 8   C. 12   D. 24

3. All of the following agencies require that Central Service employees have been properly trained and competent in their job EXCEPT 3._____
    A. Joint Commission
    B. Centers of Medicare and Medicaid Services
    C. Occupational Safety and Health Administration
    D. Department of Environmental Protection

4. Which of the following parameters is NOT required to be documented for every run of a sterilizer cycle? 4._____
    A. Sterilizer temperature
    B. Room temperature
    C. Cycle time
    D. Name of Central Service Technician running the cycle

5. If you are asked to decontaminate an area that could possibly be contaminated with HIV, you should allow the area to be wet with disinfectant for a minimum time of _____ seconds. 5._____
    A. 30   B. 60   C. 120   D. 300

6. If you are asked to decontaminate an area that could possibly be contaminated with HIV, you should allow the area to be wet with disinfectant for a minimum time of _____ minute(s). 6._____
    A. 1   B. 3   C. 5   D. 10

7. As of January 1, 2015, which product is NOT permitted to be used in Central Service Departments? 7._____
    A. Ethylene oxide   B. Hydrogen peroxide
    C. Oxyfume   D. Ozone

8. If a product and its associated label contains an EPA registration number, this means that the product has been deemed 8._____
    A. hazardous   B. a carcinogen
    C. safe for use   D. not for humans

9. Which of the following is the MOST appropriate definition of the role of the Central Service Technician?
   A. To provide dependable service to enhance patient care
   B. To provide sterilization services on a rigid schedule
   C. To provide the delivery of supplies
   D. To provide direct patient care

10. Medical-grade kraft paper CANNOT be used with which type of sterilization process?
    A. Steam
    B. Ozone
    C. Ethylene oxide
    D. Low temperature gas plasma

11. During cycle counts, how are items that are infrequently used but have a high dollar amount classified?
    A. A   B. B   C. C   D. D

12. Which of the following sets would be considered high risk for special prion processing?
    A. Abdominal   B. Laparotomy   C. Open heart   D. Craniotomy

13. When dealing with rigid containers, which of the following testings defines the sterilizer's ability to perform under actual conditions?
    A. Biological   B. Small load   C. Chemical   D. Maximum load

14. Which of the following statements is TRUE regarding capsules?
    A. Easier to eliminate than vegetative bacteria
    B. Harder to eliminate than spores
    C. Resistant to heat and chemicals
    D. Easily eliminated by antibiotics

15. Spongiform encephalopathy is caused by
    A. fungi   B. prions   C. viruses   D. spores

16. If contamination has been removed from an item but further processing is still required, the item is said to be
    A. cleaned   B. disinfected   C. sterilized   D. sanitized

17. Which of the following should occur PRIOR to cleaning and processing a medical device?
    A. Device should be examined for proper function.
    B. Obtain approval from biomedical engineer.
    C. Material compatibility testing must be performed.
    D. Manufacturer's instructions must be obtained.

18. For what reason do alkaline detergents work BEST for mechanical washers?
    A. Extended dry cycles
    B. Lack of friction during washing
    C. Can break down proteins
    D. Compatible with high water temperatures

19. A(n) _____ detergent would be used to remove severe stains from stainless steel instruments.
    A. organic acid
    B. organic alkaline
    C. proteolytic enzyme
    D. lipolytic enzyme

20. Which of the following would be the BEST method for preventing biofilm formation on instruments?
    A. Use a metal bristled brush
    B. Use a chlorine-based cleaner
    C. Soak overnight in an enzyme solution
    D. Rinse with distilled water and dry

21. Which of the following would be the APPROPRIATE mechanical washer process to reduce the potential for corrosion?
    A. Alkaline wash, regular rinse, acid rinse
    B. Alkaline wash, acid rinse, regular rinse
    C. Regular rinse, alkaline wash, acid rinse
    D. Acid rinse, alkaline wash, regular rinse

22. What is the PROPER protocol for dealing with opened instruments that have not been used?
    Instruments should be
    A. repackaged and resterilized
    B. resterilized
    C. resterilized after the indictors have been changed
    D. completely reprocessed

23. What is the purpose of a tungsten carbide insert on a needle holder?
    A. To provide from friction than stainless steel
    B. To hold the suture needle better
    C. To grip smaller needles
    D. To allow for easier cleanliness inspections

24. What is the PROPER action if the temperature in the central service area is 70°F and the humidity is 69%?
    A. Humidity must be increased.
    B. Temperature must be lowered.
    C. All packages must be inspected for moisture.
    D. Continue with normal activities.

25. Which of the following statements is TRUE regarding individuals entering the preparation area?
    A. All individuals must sign in
    B. Must be an employee of the facility
    C. Must wear proper attire
    D. Must be at least 21 years of age

KEY (CORRECT ANSWERS)

1. A
2. B
3. D
4. B
5. A

6. D
7. C
8. C
9. A
10. D

11. A
12. D
13. D
14. C
15. B

16. A
17. D
18. B
19. A
20. D

21. B
22. D
23. B
24. D
25. C

TEST 5

DIRECTIONS: Each question or incomplete statement is followed by several suggested answers or completions. Select the one that BEST answers the question or completes the statement. *PRINT THE LETTER OF THE CORRECT ANSWER IN THE SPACE AT THE RIGHT.*

1. If a wrapper is to be used as a sterile field, how far over the table must it extend?
   A. 1 inch B. 2 inches C. 4 inches D. 6 inches

   1.____

2. Rigid containers are considered to be a medical device and must have a 510k clearance from which agency?
   A. Environmental Protection Agency
   B. Food and Drug Administration
   C. Centers for Disease Control and Prevention
   D. World Health Organization

   2.____

3. Which of the following actions can eliminate the need for frequent instrument reprocessing?
   A. Establishing minimum stock quantities
   B. Using plastic bags for dust covers
   C. Ordering additional supplies
   D. Proper stock rotation

   3.____

4. Which of the following is the MOST important element involved with double peel pouching?
   A. The inner pouch must lay flat inside the outer pouch.
   B. The two pouches should be sealed together.
   C. The inner package must remain unsealed.
   D. The inner package should be folded to fit inside the outer pouch.

   4.____

5. Which of the following is the INITIAL step that should be taken with an instrument needs to be sterilized for immediate use?
   A. Instrument should be wrapped in a double thickness non-woven wrap.
   B. Biological indicator should be placed in the sterilizer.
   C. Instrument should be cleaned according to manufacturer's specifications.
   D. Instrument should be placed and sealed in a peel pouch.

   5.____

6. _____ will result if air has not been removed from a package within a steam sterilizer.
   A. Non-adherence of autoclave tape   B. Wet packs
   C. Drying of packaging material   D. Poor steam penetration

   6.____

7. Name the instrument in the illustration shown at the right.
   A. Rongeur
   B. Screwdriver
   C. Osteotome
   D. Scoville retractor

7.____

8. Which of the following actions can be taken to avoid damage to medical/ surgical supplies in the receiving area?
   A. Removing supplies from the original shipping cartons
   B. Avoiding temperature and humidity extremes
   C. Storing supplies at least 8 inches off the floor
   D. Storing supplies at least 18 inches off the ceiling

8.____

9.

9.____

The instrument in the above illustration is used for what purpose?
   A. Vascular procedures to avoid tissue damage
   B. Widen tracheal incisions
   C. Gouging out bone
   D. Scraping or debriding biological tissue

10. Through what area is steam exhausted from the sterilizer?
    A. Chamber jacket   B. Chamber drain line
    C. Door gasket   D. Pressure gauge

10.____

11. For what reason should textile packs be placed on their side during the sterilization process?
    A. To facilitate the drying process
    B. To facilitate air removal and steam penetration
    C. To allow for the maximum number of packs to be loaded
    D. For better response from chemical indicators

11.____

12. What is the process employed by ethylene oxide to eliminate the presence of microorganisms?
    A. Cavitation   B. Oxidation
    C. Alkylation   D. Passivation

12.____

13. Which of the following represents the normal concentration of hydrogen peroxide in a low temperature gas plasma sterilizer?
    A. 27% B. 46% C. 59% D. 78%

14. Name the instrument in the illustration shown at the right.
    A. Weitlander Retractor
    B. Balfour Retractor
    C. Bookwalter Retractor
    D. Hibbs Retractor

15. Rigid sterilization containers should be biologically tested prior to
    A. purchasing
    B. testing the gaskets
    C. the placement of filters
    D. the first cycle of the day

16. Which of the following represents the optimum amount of a supply to order?
    A. Economical order quantity
    B. Perpetual inventory count
    C. Cycle count
    D. Reorder point

17. Which of the following terms is synonymous with par level inventory?
    A. Total exchange cart
    B. Demand distribution
    C. Just in time distribution
    D. Fixed inventory level

18. Which distribution system is designed to reduce storeroom inventory?
    A. Just in time
    B. Exchange carts
    C. Par level inventory
    D. Demand distribution

19. An exhaust hood over the ethylene oxide sterilizer is an example of a(n) _____ control.
    A. environmental
    B. emission
    C. biological
    D. engineering

20. If a chemical indicator responds to two or more critical parameters, it belongs to Class
    A. 2 B. 3 C. 4 D. 5

21. What is the PROPER method in which to place paper/plastic pouches in a sterilizer?
    A. Paper facing paper in a basket
    B. Plastic facing plastic in a basket
    C. Paper facing plastic in a basket
    D. On their edge between other packages

22. The instrument in the illustration shown at the right is used for what purpose?
    A. Severe scalp lacerations
    B. Clamp blood vessels
    C. Cut tissue
    D. Retract soft tissue

22._____

23. For what reason is it important to evenly distribute large instruments in a set?
    A. Make the set easier to carry
    B. Make the set easier to sort
    C. Make the set easier to dry
    D. Provide a more thorough sterilization

23._____

24. The MINIMUM length of time central service technicians should scrub their hands during washing is _____ seconds.
    A. 15   B. 30   C. 45   D. 60

24._____

25. Instrument marking tape should be wrapped around an instrument _____ times.
    A. 1-1.5   B. 2-2.5   C. 3-3.5   D. 4-4.5

25._____

KEY (CORRECT ANSWERS)

1.	D	11.	B
2.	B	12.	C
3.	D	13.	C
4.	A	14.	C
5.	C	15.	B
6.	D	16.	A
7.	C	17.	D
8.	A	18.	A
9.	A	19.	D
10.	B	20.	C

21. C
22. A
23. C
24. A
25. A

TEST 6

DIRECTIONS: Each question or incomplete statement is followed by several suggested answers or completions. Select the one that BEST answers the question or completes the statement. *PRINT THE LETTER OF THE CORRECT ANSWER IN THE SPACE AT THE RIGHT.*

1. Patients, visitors, and vendors are considered to be what kind of customers to the central service department?
    A. Internal customers
    B. External customers
    C. Exclusive customer
    D. Professional customers

    1.____

2. Surgeons, emergency rooms, and endoscopy suites are considered to be what kind of customers to the central service department?
    A. Internal customers
    B. External customers
    C. Exclusive customer
    D. Professional customers

    2.____

3. Which of the following would be considered a vendor concern?
    A. Employee education
    B. Employee efficiency
    C. Availability of product
    D. Quality of product

    3.____

4. Which of the following would be considered a labor concern?
    A. Product repeatability
    B. Employee education
    C. Availability of product
    D. Quality of product

    4.____

5. _____ is at the heart of any process to facilitate customer service.
    A. Common courtesy
    B. Mutual respect
    C. Shared vision
    D. Effective communication

    5.____

6. Which of the five dimensions of service quality assessment includes the appearance of physical facilities, equipment, personnel, and communication materials?
    A. Tangibles
    B. Reliability
    C. Responsiveness
    D. Assurance

    6.____

7. Which of the five dimensions of service quality assessment involves the knowledge and courtesy of employees and their ability to convey trust and confidence?
    A. Empathy
    B. Reliability
    C. Responsiveness
    D. Assurance

    7.____

8. _____ are used to prevent the formation of blood clots.
    A. Sequential compression devices
    B. Continuous passive motion devices
    C. Patient controlled analgesia pumps
    D. Hypo/hyperemia machines

    8.____

9. Which of the following is an example of a flexible endoscope?
   A. Cystoscope
   B. Bronchoscope
   C. Arthroscope
   D. Resectoscope

10. Which of the following statements is FALSE regarding labeling packages?
    A. For packs, labeling should be on the indicator tape not on the wrapper.
    B. For peel pouches, labeling should be on the plastic side of the pouch.
    C. Marking pen should contain nontoxic permanent ink.
    D. Label after sterilization to insure sterility.

11. _____ is defined as the number of microorganisms on a contaminated object.
    A. Biofilm
    B. Bioburden
    C. Biological indicator
    D. Biohazard

12. Which of the following is defined as the transport of heat from a location of higher temperature to an area of lower temperature by a flow or current of liquids or gases?
    A. Circulation
    B. Convection
    C. Transference
    D. Translocation

13. _____ is the process in which a substance produces a chemical reaction that causes a physical change in the material.
    A. Corrosion
    B. Convection
    C. Cavitation
    D. Passivation

14. A device entering sterile tissue is referred to as a _____ device.
    A. critical
    B. non-critical
    C. semi-critical
    D. hyper-critical

15. _____ is the process in which air is removed from water in an ultrasonic cleaner.
    A. Deionization
    B. Degassing
    C. Impingement
    D. Denaturing

16. Which of the following is a microorganism used to biologically monitor steam, low-temperature gas plasma, and paracetic acid sterilizers?
    A. Geobacillus stearothermophilus
    B. Clostridium difficile
    C. Methacillin-resistant Staphylococcus aureus
    D. Vancomycin-resistant enterococci

17. Which of the following is a high level disinfectant that can achieve high level disinfection in a 12-minute exposure time when used for manual immersion at room temperature, or in a 5-minute exposure time when used in an automated endoscope reprocessor?
    A. Glutaraldehyde
    B. Formaldehyde
    C. Ortho-phthaldehyde
    D. Paraldehyde

18. _____ is a process of heating fluid to a moderate temperature for a specific period of time to destroy bacteria without changing the chemical composition of the fluid.
    A. Passivation
    B. Oxidation
    C. Pasteurization
    D. Cavitation

19. Steam that contains 3% entrained water is referred to as _____ steam.
    A. saturated
    B. distilled
    C. hydrolyzed
    D. entrenched

20. A device that comes into contact with the mucous membranes is referred to as a _____ device.
    A. critical
    B. non-critical
    C. semi-critical
    D. hyper-critical

21. The use of two separate layers of wrapping material to create a package within a package is referred to as _____ wrapping.
    A. serial
    B. simultaneous
    C. sequential
    D. standardized

22. _____ steam is defined as water vapor in a state of equilibrium between condensation and evaporation.
    A. saturated
    B. distilled
    C. hydrolyzed
    D. superheated

23. A table-top sterilizer has a chamber volume of no more than _____ cubic feet.
    A. 2
    B. 3
    C. 4
    D. 5

24. The instrument shown above is used for what purpose?
    A. Vascular procedures to avoid tissue damage
    B. Widen tracheal incisions
    C. Gouging out bone
    D. Scraping or debriding biological tissue

25. Which of the following is an inanimate object that serves as a transmission agent for microorganisms?
    A. Prion
    B. Fomite
    C. Aerobe
    D. Antigen

KEY (CORRECT ANSWERS)

1.	B	11.	B
2.	A	12.	B
3.	C	13.	A
4.	B	14.	A
5.	D	15.	B
6.	A	16.	A
7.	D	17.	C
8.	A	18.	C
9.	B	19.	A
10.	D	20.	C

21.	C
22.	D
23.	A
24.	C
25.	B

STERILANTS AND DISINFECTANTS IN HEALTHCARE FACILITIES

In a healthcare setting, it is essential to be able to control infectious organisms. Sterilants and disinfectants are important tools for meeting that need. But because they are necessarily toxic to living organisms, sterilants and disinfectants must be handled carefully, and their associated wastes must be managed properly, to avoid causing unintentional harm as they fulfill their intended function. These page provide an introduction to sterilants and disinfectants in common use, and include information on proper handling and disposal, and on available alternatives.

The information presented below applies primarily to sterilizing and disinfecting medical devices and other items that may contact patients.

- Properties
- Risks
- Compliance requirements
- Alternatives
- Disposal of sterilant and disinfectant wastes

Properties

Sterilants and disinfectants kill living organisms. They need that essential property to perform their basic function. But "desirable" organisms (like us, presumably), and "undesirable" organisms, like disease-causing pathogens, are not that different at the cellular level, where their basic metabolic processes are concerned. If a substance is toxic to pathogens, chances are it will also be harmful to other organisms.

While all sterilants and disinfectants are toxic to some degree, some have greater killing power than others. High toxicity is an advantage in critical applications, where the risk of infection must be reduced to the lowest possible level. But the greater effectiveness of highly toxic materials comes at a price:

- the risk of harm to staff and patients through inadvertent exposure will be greater
- the disposal of wastes from disinfection processes may become more difficult and costly

Healthcare professionals have developed two interrelated classification systems to help determine appropriate infection control materials for various clinical situations. One system is concerned with classifying **levels of infection risk** -- in other words, with providing "how clean is clean?" guidelines based on plausible exposure risks. The other system is concerned with classifying **levels of effective potency** of disinfection materials. Using the two systems, you can match the material with the need, and ensure a safe level of infection control without overkill -- i.e. without overusing materials that pose needless risks of their own, and increase your costs as well.

Categories of Infection Risk

According to one commonly used scheme, infection risk situations are divided into three categories:

- **Critical:** contact directly with internal fluids, such as with circulating blood though blood vessel walls, or contact directly with tissues through broken skin
- **Semi-critical:** contact with mucous membranes, or contact with broken skin
- **Noncritical:** contact with intact skin

Categories of Effective Potency

Sterilants and disinfectants are distinguished according to the degree to which they can be expected to destroy the organisms they contact:

- **Sterilants** are capable of completely eliminating or destroying all forms of microbial life, including spores.
- **Disinfectants** form a less absolute category -- they will destroy some, but not necessarily all organisms. The category is further divided into subcategories, as follows:
    - **High-level disinfectants** - destroy all microorganisms, with the exception of high numbers of bacterial spores.
    - **Intermediate-level disinfectants** - inactivate even resistant organisms such as *Mycobacterium* tuberculosis, as well as vegetative bacteria, most viruses, and most fungi, but do not necessarily kill bacterial spores.
    - **Low-level disinfectants** - kill most bacteria, some viruses, and some fungi, but cannot be relied on to kill resistant microorganisms such as tubercle bacilli or bacterial spores. (Source: APIC.)

Choosing the appropriate material to match risk with potency

- Any objects or materials used where the risk of infection is **critical** should be absolutely sterile.
- For **semi-critical** risk situations, either a high-level or a medium-level disinfectant may be appropriate, depending on the type of exposure. For example, a publication from the Association for Professionals in Infection Control and Epidemiology (APIC) recommends high-level disinfectants for devices like laryngoscopes and endoscopes that are inserted deep into body cavities, and medium-level disinfectants for less intrusive devices such as oral or rectal thermometers.
- For **noncritical** risk situations, low-level disinfectants may be adequate.

The most widely used sterilants and disinfectants in healthcare facilities are:

- **Ethylene oxide (EtO).** Hospitals typically use ethylene oxide (EtO) to sterilize moisture- and heat-sensitive instruments. EtO is a hazardous air pollutant (HAP) and the operation of EtO sterilizers is regulated by a National Emission Standard for Hazardous Air Pollutants (for guidance on how to comply see: EPA guidance document Summary of Regulations Controlling Air Emissions from the Hospital Sterilizers Using Ethylene Oxide).
- **Glutaraldehyde.** Glutaraldehyde is a high-level disinfectant most frequently used as a disinfectant for heat-sensitive equipment such as dialysis instruments, surgical

instruments, suction bottles, bronchoscopes, endoscopes, and ear, nose, and throat instruments. Glutaraldehyde is also used as a tissue fixative in histology and pathology laboratories and as a hardening agent in the development of x-rays. Glutaraldehyde products are marketed under a variety of brand names and are available in a variety of concentrations (solutions range in concentration from 2.4 – 3.4%), with and without surfactants.

Both of these materials have been found to cause potential problems for facility staff and for any other individuals who may be exposed to them (see the following section). Alternatives are available for most applications (see the Alternatives section below).

Note that there are also non-chemical methods of sterilizing and disinfecting that may be suitable in some cases:

- Some methods rely on high heat and pressure, such as the conditions obtainable in an autoclave. Since boiling in water is not sufficient for sterilization -- some particularly hardy spores can survive exposure to the temperature at which water boils under normal atmospheric pressure -- more drastic conditions are needed to sterilize without the use of biotoxic chemicals. Autoclaves are enclosed chambers that operate under increased pressure, allowing water to remain liquid at temperatures well above its normal boiling point. This can provide a very effective sterilization environment. However, autoclaving is not an option for heat sensitive equipment.
- Radiation can also be used for sterilizing and disinfecting, but considering its own well-known suite of problems, it would not generally be considered a preferable alternative to chemical methods from an environmental and safety standpoint.

Risks

(Note -- this section deals with the risks involved in using and disposing of the most commonly used sterilants and disinfectants. The risks associated with infection are surveyed in the previous section.)

Ethylene oxide (EtO) poses several health hazards requiring special handling and disposal of the chemical, and training in its use. It is identified by the National Toxicology Program as a known human carcinogen and has several other acute and chronic health effects. Ethylene oxide:

- can cause nausea, vomiting, and neurological disorders
- in solution, can severely irritate and burn the skin, eyes, and lungs
- acts as a probable teratogen, and may pose reproductive hazards
- may damage the central nervous system, liver, and kidneys, or cause cataracts
- is extremely reactive and flammable, increasing the risk of chemical accidents that could injure hospital employees and patients

(Source: Replacing Ethylene Oxide and Glutaraldehyde, USEPA)

Glutaraldehyde is not a human carcinogen. However, several health effects have been reported among healthcare workers exposed to glutaraldehyde:

- asthma, and breathing difficulties

- burning eyes and conjunctivitis
- headaches
- nosebleed, irritation, sneezing, and wheezing
- hives
- nausea
- rashes and allergic dermatitis
- staining of the hands
- throat and lung irritation

(Source: Glutaraldehyde: Occupational Hazards in Hospitals, CDC)

Compliance requirements

Several Occupational Safety and Health Administration (OSHA) regulations relate to sterilants and disinfectants:

- OSHA has established a permissible exposure limit (PEL) standard for ethylene oxide of 1 ppm in air as an 8 hour time weighted average, and 5 ppm over any 15 minute sampling period.
- OSHA's Hazard Communication Standard (HazCom), requires that information concerning any associated health or physical hazards be transmitted to employees via comprehensive hazard communication programs (Go to HERC HazCom page). The programs must include:
    - **Written Program.** A written that meets the requirements of the Hazard Communication Standard (HazCom).
    - **Labels.** In-plant containers of hazardous chemicals must be labeled, tagged, or marked with the identity of the material and appropriate hazard warnings.
    - **Material Safety Data Sheets.** Employers must have an MSDS for each hazardous chemical which they use and MSDSs must be readily accessible to employees when they are in their work areas during their workshifts.
    - **Employee Information and Training**. Each employee who may be "exposed" to hazardous chemicals when working must be provided information and be trained prior to initial assignment to work with a hazardous chemical, and whenever the hazard changes.
- Depending on the ingredients contained in a sterilant or disinfectant and its manner of use, employee protection may be required, including:
    - ventilation controls
    - personal protective equipment
    - clothing or gloves

and other applicable precautions. This assessment should be made by the employer, again, based on the unique conditions of use of the product at that establishment.

- Where the eyes or body of any person may be exposed to injurious corrosive materials, **employers must provide** suitable mechanisms for quick drenching or flushing of the eyes and body within the work area for immediate emergency use [1910.151(c)].

Certain Environmental Protection Agency (EPA) regulations may also apply to sterilants and disinfectants:

- On December 20, 2007, the EPA issued nationwide standards (NESHAP Subpart WWWWW) to reduce emissions of ethylene oxide (EtO) from hospital sterilizers. This regulation requires hospitals to implement a management practice to reduce ethylene oxide emissions by sterilizing full loads to the extent practicable. Hospitals which route ethylene oxide to a control device are in compliance with the rule requirements. Existing sources must be in compliance by December 29, 2008. New sources (construction after Nov. 6, 2006) must be in compliance at the time of startup. Affected hospitals must submit a Notification of Compliance Status (INOCS) within 180 days after their compliance date (for guidance on how to comply see: EPA guidance document Summary of Regulations Controlling Air Emissions from the Hospital Sterilizers Using Ethylene Oxide).
- The Federal Insecticide, Fungicide and Rodenticide Act (FIFRA) provides EPA with the authority to oversee the registration, distribution, sale and use of pesticides. FIFRA applies to all types of pesticides, including antimicrobials, which includes sterilants, disinfectants and other cleaning compounds that are intended to control microorganisms on surfaces. FIFRA requires users of products to follow the labeling directions on each product explicitly. (go to FIFRA page).
- Discarded sterilants and disinfectants may be a hazardous waste due to their corrosiveness, flammability, toxicity, or reactivity. For information on how to properly identify your hazardous waste, please see HERC's Hazardous Waste Determination page. You should also check the HERC Hazardous Waste State Resource Locator page for your state for links to any state-specific variations on the federal rules that may apply to you.

Some sterilants and disinfectants are considered hazardous wastes, and are regulated under RCRA (see below).

A brief summary of which federal agency plays what role in the regulation of sterilants and disinfectants can be found in a document from the Centers for Disease Control.

Alternatives

Because of the health and environmental hazards associated with glutaraldehyde and ethylene oxide, various alternatives have been investigated. This section lists several sterilants and high level disinfectants that have been cleared by the Food and Drug Administration (FDA) for processing reusable medical and dental devices along with specific references to some commercially available products.

The list is provided for your convenience, and is not intended to provide specific recommendations. In general, when selecting an alternative, you should choose a disinfectant that is sufficiently effective, but is the least toxic to employees and the environment.

Here are a few general observations.

- Disinfectants that act by generating active forms of oxygen, such as hydrogen peroxide or peracetic acid, typically create fewer by-products than compounds relying on other active elements, such as chlorine or the form of nitrogen found in quaternary amine compounds. This means fewer toxins finding their way to the sewer.
- Hydrogen peroxide and peracetic acid are less easily inactivated by other, noninfectious organic matter than some of the non-oxygen disinfectants.

- Hydrogen peroxide and peracetic acid can be effective against a broader range of infectious agents than some of the other alternatives.

Under any circumstances, when alternatives sterilants and disinfectants are to be used on a medical device, you should check with the original equipment manufacturer for any specific warranty restrictions on the use of specific materials or methods of disinfection.

Hydrogen peroxide provides high level disinfection in 30 minutes at 20 degrees Celsius. Although the FDA has approved products containing 7.5% hydrogen peroxide as a high-level disinfectant/sterilant, it has not been found to be compatible with all flexible gastrointestinal endoscopes (e.g., Olympus, Pentax or Fujinon). Available products include:

- **Sporox™ Sterilizing & Disinfection Solution,** Sultan Chemists, (7.5% hydrogen peroxide)
- Sterrad™ Sterilization Systems, Johnson & Johnson, (hydrogen peroxide plasma)

Peracetic acid is part of the family of peryoxygen compounds. A concentration of 0.2% peracetic acid is rapidly active against all microorganisms including bacterial spores, and is effective in the presence of organic matter. It has proved to be an acceptable alternative to EtO. FDA cleared products include:

- **STERIS 20™ Sterilant** (*Cleared for use with the STERIS System 1™ Processor only.*), STERIS™ Corporation, **0.2% peracetic acid.**

However, you should note that in some instances, manufacturers have not yet approved the use of EtO alternatives for sterilization of their products. Such limitations vary by vendor and are not specific to one instrument or medical device product type. For example, one typical hospital has investigated EtO alternatives, but still requires the use of EtO on the following five instruments:

- angioscopes
- choledocoscopes
- surgiscopes
- bone flaps
- hysterectoscopes.

(Source: Replacing Ethylene Oxide and Glutaraldehyde, USEPA).

Peracetic Acid-Hydrogen Peroxide mixtures. Although the FDA has approved products containing 0.08% Peracetic Acid/1% Hydrogen Peroxide as a high-level disinfectant/sterilant, it has not been found to be compatible with flexible gastrointestinal endoscopes manufactured by Olympus, Pentax or Fujinon. FDA cleared products include:

- **Acecide™ High Level Disinfectant and Sterilant,** Minntech Corp., 8.3% hydrogen peroxide 7.0% peracetic acid,
- **EndoSpor™ Plus Sterilizing and Disinfecting Solution,** Cottrell Limited, 7.35% hydrogen peroxide 0.23% peracetic acid
- **Peract™ 20 Liquid Sterilant/Disinfectant,** Minntech Corp., 1.0% hydrogen peroxide, 0.08% peracetic acid

Hypochlorite has FDA clearance for high level disinfection in 10 minutes at 25 degrees Celsius. FDA cleared products include:

- **Sterilox Liquid High Level Disinfectant System,** Sterilox, Technologies, Inc., hypochlorite and hypochlorous acid, 650-675 ppm active free chlorine.

Ortho-phthalaldehyde (OPA) is chemically related to glutaraldehyde. According to the Michigan Health and Hospital Association (MHA), the disinfecting mechanism of OPA is thought to be similar to glutaraldehyde and is based on the powerful binding of the aldehyde to the outer cell wall of contaminant organisms. A notable difference between the two commercial disinfectants is the percent of active ingredient in each product. Commercial OPA-based disinfecting products contain only 0.55% of the active ingredient, while most glutaraldehyde-based disinfecting products contain 2.4 to 3.2% active ingredient – 5 to 7 times that of OPA products. is a widely used glutaraldehyde alternative. Its potential benefits include:

- lower inhalation exposure risk,
- reduced disinfecting time (12 minutes vs. APIC-approved 20 minute disinfection time and FDA-approved 45 minute disinfecting time for Cidex),
- solution is approved for use in almost all of their equipment without negating the warranty, and
- cost is significantly less than installing a more substantial ventilation system to minimize respiratory irritation from using glutaraldehyde.

Ortho-phthalaldehyde is a clear blue solution with little odor. It is a potential irritant of eyes, skin, nose and other tissues resulting in symptoms such as stinging, excessive tearing, coughing and sneezing. It is a potential skin and respiratory sensitizer that may cause dermatitis with prolonged or repeated contact and may aggravate pre-existing bronchitis or asthma. In addition, the product stains proteins on surfaces to gray/black. Although OPA may pose similar occupational hazards to glutaraldehyde, the risk is significantly reduced due to the low percentage of OPA and relatively low vapor pressure of OPA-based commercial products. OPA does not currently have a recommended exposure limit; however, vendors recommend that similar protective equipment be used, including gloves and goggles. (Source: Replacing Ethylene Oxide and Glutaraldehyde, USEPA). FDA cleared products include:

- **Cidex OPA Concentrate,** Advanced Sterilization Products, (5.75% *ortho*-phthalaldehyde)
- **Cidex OPA Solution,** Advanced Sterilization Products, (0.55% *ortho*-phthalaldehyde)

Disposal of sterilant and disinfectant wastes

Unused disinfectant concentrates may be considered hazardous wastes in some cases. If so, they need to be managed under a particular set of rules (RCRA). You should also to check to see if the end product being used (i.e. the product after dilution) also needs to be managed under RCRA.

Here are a few considerations:

- If the sole active ingredient of a sterilant or disinfectant is a P or U-listed waste, the product itself must be managed as a hazardous waste. (This information should be

available on the Material Safety Data Sheet (MSDS) that your supplier can provide for the product.)
- A sterilant or disinfectant might also have to be considered a <u>characteristic hazardous waste</u> due to:
    - <u>corrosivity</u>: It is important to check the pH level of the product. Many products have pHs higher than 11 or lower than 2. A sterilant or disinfectant product may be considered hazardous if it has a pH of less than 2 or greater than 12.5. This information can be determined form the MSDS under the "Physical Data" category.
    - <u>toxicity</u>
    - <u>reactivity</u>

See the <u>Hazardous Waste Determination page</u> for more background information on this topic.

Some solutions can be disposed of to the sanitary sewer if the local POTW permits it. You are strongly advised to check with your POTW to determine what wastewater discharges of sterilants and disinfectants are acceptable.

A note on the disposal of ortho-phthalaldehyde (OPA)-containing products: Due to its toxicity, California legislation deemed Cidex OPA a hazardous waste beginning January 1, 2001. However, this legislation exempts healthcare facilities from tiered permitting regulatory requirements when treating Cidex OPA with glycine on site to render it a non hazardous waste. Note also that if local publicly owned treatment works (POTWs) or sewer agencies have other prohibitions against sewerage of aldehydes, facilities must seek approval for this process as well. (Source: <u>Replacing Ethylene Oxide and Glutaraldehyde</u>, USEPA)

BASIC FUNDAMENTALS OF MICROBIOLOGY, STERILIZATION, DISINFECTION, AND ASEPTIC TECHNIQUE

CONTENTS

	Page
SECTION A - Microbiology	1
SECTION B - Sterilization	2
SECTION C - Processing Supplies for Sterilization	6
SECTION D - Disinfection	8
SECTION E - Aseptic Technique	11

BASIC FUNDAMENTALS OF MICROBIOLOGY, STERILIZATION, DISINFECTION, AND ASEPTIC TECHNIQUE

SECTION A—MICROBIOLOGY

1. Introduction. The activities so often associated with operating room scenes have a very definite purpose. It took a long time for man to understand the cause of infection and to develop methods for preventing it. The science which evolved about the subject is called "microbiology." Microbiology is the study of living things which are of microscopic size. These microorganisms include bacteria, viruses, fungi (molds and yeasts), and animal parasites (worms and protozoa). A knowledge of the basic principles of microbiology is necessary for a clear understanding of the environmental activities carried out in the operating suite.

2. Identification and Classification of Microorganisms. Microorganisms are minute, living structures that are categorized as plants, animals, or viruses. Bacteria are one-celled plants which differ from animal cells. The plant cell has a cell wall made of cellulose in addition to a cell membrane. However, many aspects of plant cells are similar to those of animal cells. These similarities include the facts that both plant and animal cells contain a nucleus and cytoplasm, and both have certain oxygen, temperature, moisture, nutritional, and pH (acid-base) requirements.

  a. A few organisms, because of their oxygen requirements, are of special concern to operating room personnel. The oxygen requirement is important because some organisms (aerobes) must have free oxygen to survive. On the other hand, anaerobes, such as those causing tetanus and gas gangrene, can only reproduce in the absence of free oxygen. Anaerobic organisms require special consideration in surgery where deep wounds offer an ideal environment for them to grow and to excrete disease-producing toxins.

  b. Not all microorganisms are pathogenic (disease-producing). There are microbes on the skin, in the mouth and nose, in the air, and on practically every object we touch. Most of these never produce disease, and many of them have useful functions in the body, as well as in the world at large. In addition, there are certain organisms which will produce disease only after they are introduced into a particular type of environment. For example, *Escherichia coli*, whose normal habitat is inside the intestine, will produce peritonitis if it ruptures through the intestinal wall. The body defenses, such as white blood cells and certain elements of plasma, fight against the invasion of foreign substances, including microorganisms, and as long as the body remains healthy, many organisms are powerless against these defenses. Once the defenses are broken down as the result of an open wound or because of a generally lowered resistance following surgery, the stage may be set for the entrance and growth of pathogenic organisms, as well as those that would ordinarily never cause any harm.

3. Spore-Forming Bacteria. Certain bacteria (*Bacillus*, for example) are capable of protecting themselves against adverse conditions by the formation of spores. Spores are round granules, which are dry and thick-walled. These granules seem to contain protoplasm in a dehydrated form. Protoplasm is the essential form of matter in which life is manifested. Bacterial spores are the most resistant form of microbial life, and they are far more capable of resisting external destructive agents and of withstanding exposure to temperature extremes than are vegetative cells. Once formed within the bacterial cell, the spore remains dormant until proper growth conditions cause it to germinate into a vegetative cell. Since this dormant period may last for years, viable spores are disseminated so widely in nature that we must assume they are present in most situations involving disinfection and sterilization in medical facilities.

4. Environmental Temperature. The lowest temperature at which a cell will grow is the "minimum temperature," while the highest temperature at which it will grow is the "maximum temperature." "Optimum temperature" is the temperature best suited for a particular organism. The "thermal death point" is that temperature which, in time, will kill all organisms present. Cells will grow and reproduce if an adequate temperature and other needs (oxygen, food, moisture, and pH) are met. ALTERING THE ENVIRONMENTAL CONDITIONS MAY DESTROY OR INHIBIT BACTERIAL GROWTH. THIS FORMS THE BASIS OF ALL SURGICAL ASEPSIS.

5. Bacterial Cultures. Bacterial cells are collected by swabbing a suspect area, using Rodac plates or collecting air samples on culture plates. Sterile, moist swabs must be used if an area is to be swabbed. The cells are then transferred to a tube of culture media or streaked on a culture plate. The tubes or plates are then incubated until the cells reproduce and form colonies which are visible to the naked eye. At this point, they also exhibit clues to the bacteriologist as to their identity. These clues are usually in the form of color, size, and shape. It is from these colonies that the bacteriologist takes samples and sets up slides that finally make microscopic identification possible.

SECTION B—STERILIZATION

6. Introduction. Since the basis for the living process in microorganisms is protein in nature, conditions that adversely affect protein will destroy these cells. Heat, chemical agents, and radiation applied in the proper manner will kill or inhibit the growth of microorganisms. The mechanisms responsible for the destruction of microorganisms are the coagulation of the protoplasmic mass or the chemical alteration of the structure of the cell. THE PROCESS WHICH DESTROYS ALL MICROORGANISMS IS CALLED STERILIZATION.

7. Methods of Sterilization. Operating room personnel should be thoroughly familiar with the various methods of sterilization. Not only should they know how to operate the sterilizing equipment, but they should also be able to select the one most effective in a given situation.

a. Steam under pressure is the most common form of sterilization used in the surgical suite. Microorganisms are destroyed by heat. However, moist heat kills bacteria faster and at a lower temperature than does dry heat. Moisture is provided by steam, and the pressure is used to assure that the steam will attain and maintain the temperature needed for sterilization. In order for the steam under pressure to produce sterility there must be direct steam contact with the item to be sterilized. Anhydrous oils, greases, and powders cannot be sterilized by steam under pressure as the steam cannot penetrate these materials. Otherwise, any item which is not heat or moisture sensitive can be sterilized in a steam-under-pressure sterilizer.

b. Dry heat (hot-air) is another method of utilizing heat for sterilization. The theory is that heat is absorbed from the surface of the substance which is being sterilized. As explained above, dry heat sterilization requires higher temperature and longer exposure time than moist heat. Hot-air sterilizers are impractical for operating room use; therefore, they are seldom available in surgical suites.

c. Gas sterilization is essentially sterilization with a chemical agent. Ethylene oxide, and other gases, are believed to interfere with the chemical make-up of microorganisms, thus rendering them incapable of biological activities. Ethylene oxide gas is used to sterilize heat-labile and moisture-sensitive materials. In addition to the time and temperature factors, gas concentration and controlled moisture also are important in ethylene oxide sterilization. Barriers to gas permeation or diffusion can create problems in attaining sterility.

d. Sterilization by radiation, while not used in hospitals, is commonly used by manufacturers to sterilize many of the prepackaged, presterilized articles used in the operating room.

8. Steam Under Pressure Sterilizers. These sterilizers are designed to hold items for sterilization and to allow steam under pressure to contact or penetrate these items. Figure 1 illustrates the basic design of a steam under pressure sterilizer. There are several types of steam sterilizers and those most widely used are discussed below.

a. *The Downward Displacement Steam Sterilizer.* After the door is closed, steam is admitted through the inlet. Since air is heavier than steam, gravity draws the air downward and outward as steam enters the chamber. This process is rapid when the sterilizer is empty, but when it is filled, air may be trapped in and around the packages causing cool air pockets which prevent the steam from contacting all portions of the contents. Once the steam has displaced the air, the outlet is closed by a heat-sensitive valve activated by the heated steam. After time is allowed for steam to penetrate to the center of linen packs, a specified time is required for sterilization. A thermometer recording system indicates and records the same temperature as that of the thermometer located at the discharge line. It records the length of each exposure cycle over a 24-hour period. The recording chart should be checked at frequent intervals to assure that the correct time and temperatures are being reached and maintained. An automatic timer gives a light or sound signal at the completion of the sterilization cycle. The steam is then exhausted from the chamber and the material is dried before being removed from the sterilizer.

b. *The Prevacuum, High-Temperature Steam Sterilizer.* This sterilizer was designed to provide a faster and more reliable method of sterilization than provided by the downward displacement steam sterilizer. Air trapped inside the sterilizing chamber is one of the greatest dangers encountered in steam-

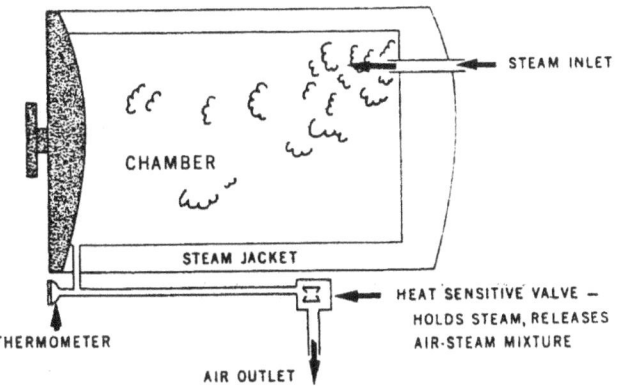

Figure 1. Steam Under Pressure Sterilizer.

under-pressure sterilization. The efficiency of the steam sterilizer is improved by pumping the air from the chamber and creating a nearly perfect vacuum before introducing steam into the chamber. This procedure allows fast and more positive steam penetration of the entire sterilizer load. The cycles of this sterilizer are relatively short due to the fact that the system removes air from the chamber with a vacuum pump and operates at temperatures of 272° F to 276° F. The sterilizing time required is shorter because of prevacuum and higher temperature. The drying time is shorter because of vacuum drying.

c. *The High-Speed, Pressure-Instrument Sterilizer (Flash Sterilizer).* This sterilizer is designed to sterilize surgical instruments. Moist heat, produced by steam under pressure, is the sterilizing agent. Unwrapped instruments which have been dropped or have been omitted from the instrument setup can be sterilized in 3 minutes in a perforated tray. For instruments in a lightly covered or padded tray, the sterilizing time is 10 minutes. Wrapped instruments require 15 minutes for sterilization as extra time is required for the steam to penetrate the fabric and for drying the wrapped packages. However, some flash sterilizers are not equipped with a vacuum dryer. Obviously, wrapped instruments cannot be sterilized in sterilizers which have no drying phase capability. If doubt exists, check the manufacturer's instructions.

d. *Instrument Washer-Sterilizer.* An instrument washer-sterilizer is a pressure vessel which automatically washes, sterilizes, and dries surgical instruments. An agitated detergent bath, which is heated by steam jets, performs the washing. Residual heat in the instruments dries any moisture which remains after the steam is exhausted. The sterilizing cycle of this sterilizer will sterilize clean, unwrapped instruments in 3 minutes. Instruments with other materials, such as suture or rubber tubing, can be sterilized in 10 minutes. This sterilizer is not suitable for sterilizing wrapped instruments as it has no drying capability.

e. *Specific Details.* Specific details for operating these sterilizers have not been included here as their operation may vary according to the manufacturer. Local operating procedures and manufacturer's instructions should be consulted for operating details.

9. Ethylene Oxide Gas Sterilization. Sterilization with ethylene oxide gas is used for articles which would be damaged by the heat or moisture in steam-under-pressure sterilizers. Gas sterilization should not be used for any article which can be steam sterilized.

a. Ethylene oxide is a colorless gas which acts as a vesicant if it comes in contact with the skin. The vapor may cause eye and nose irritation, and overexposure can lead to nausea, vomiting, and dizziness. It is highly flammable and when mixed with air can be ignited by electric spark, static electricity, open flame, or other heat- or spark-producing conditions.

b. To overcome the toxic and flammable properties of ethylene oxide gas, it is mixed with an inert gas, such as carbon dioxide or fluorinated hydrocarbons. These mixtures are relatively safe when correctly used in properly constructed sterilizers.

c. Gas sterilizers look similar to steam sterilizers, but the conditions which produce sterility depend on the concentration of gas and humidity as well as time and temperature. Air is withdrawn from the chamber, and gas is forced in under pressure. The temperature and humidity are then brought to specified levels and held constant for the duration of the sterilizing period. Gas sterilizers must be operated by skilled personnel strictly in accordance with the instructions provided by the manufacturer.

d. Residual ethylene oxide and its byproducts, ethylene glycol and ethylene chlorhydrin, are toxic substances which can remain with articles sterilized by ethylene oxide gas. For this reason, adequate aeration time must be allowed following sterilization to reduce these residuals to a safe level. Aeration may be accomplished in a well-ventilated room. However, a faster and more efficient method is to have specially designed aeration cabinets which provide systematic air changes. Aeration time will be influenced by the type of material as well as the bulk and permeability of the items.

e. Following the manufacturer's instructions is extremely important in the overall process of ethylene oxide sterilization. A copy of the operating instructions should be affixed to each sterilizer and referred to prior to operating the sterilizer and aerating the material. In addition, manufacturer's instructions regarding resterilization of commercially prepared items must be adhered to; for example, articles containing polyvinylchloride which have

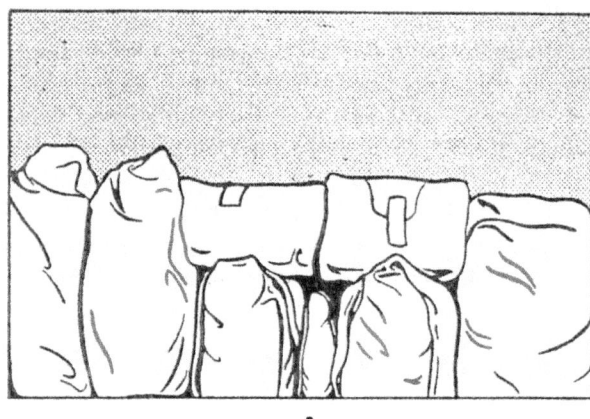

A

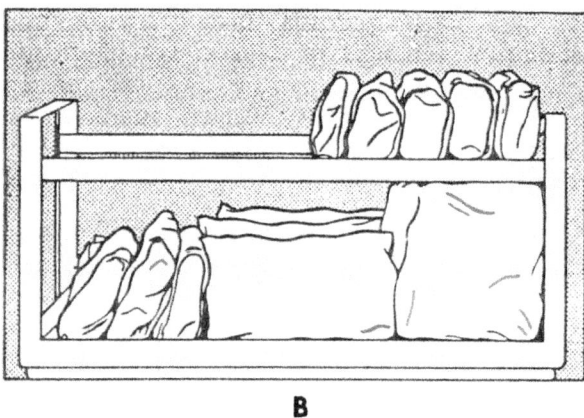

B

Figure 2. Loading Linen Packs and Packages.

been sterilized by gamma radiation must not be resterilized with ethylene oxide as it causes a chemical reaction which produces polychlorhydrin. Polychlordydrin causes toxic reactions to body tissues.

10. Loading the Sterilizer. The integrity of sterilization relies to a great extent on the correct loading of the sterilizer. The steam or gas must be allowed to flow in, around, and out of the articles or packages being sterilized.

a. Packs must be loosely wrapped and not exceed 12 by 12 by 20 inches and 12 pounds in weight.

b. The load should be arranged with the least possible resistance to the free passage of air from all areas of the chamber.

c. The sterilizer must not be overloaded or crowded. The passage of steam or gas from the top to the bottom and around the sides of the chamber must not be blocked.

d. Place all packages on edge, with large linen packs at the bottom and small packages in an upper layer crosswise to the lower layer, as illustrated in figure 2.

e. Utensils (such as pans and basin sets) should be arranged on their sides or edges in positions which allow the air to "spill" out.

f. Articles which require the same type of sterilization (gas or steam) and the same time and temperature may be sterilized together.

g. Fluids must be sterilized separately using slow vacuum to release the steam as high vacuum will pull liquids out of their containers. In vacuum sterilizers, the load is not vacuumed after the exposure time.

11. Errors in Sterilization. Usually errors which cause sterilization failures originate with people. Those errors of primary importance are:

a. Failure to observe and understand the regulation of the sterilizer so that saturated steam is maintained at sterilizing temperature.

b. Incorrect methods of packaging and wrapping supplies.

c. Carelessness in loading the sterilizer, including disregard for the necessity of providing for complete air removal and for free penetration of steam throughout the load.

d. Failure to time the exposure period correctly.

e. Removing wrapped supplies from the sterilizer while they are wet.

f. Equipment which is faulty because it has not been inspected regularly and maintained properly.

12. Sterilization Indicators. There are several ways to keep a constant check on the proper functioning of the sterilizer and to ensure efficient sterilization. Mechanical controls are used to regulate physical conditions in the sterilizer, while the thermal and biological controls test the efficiency within the load that is being processed.

a. Mechanical indicators are devices which are used to assist in identifying and preventing malfunctions and operational errors in the sterilizer.

(1) Indicating thermometers measure the temperature in the sterilizer discharge line throughout the sterilizing cycle. They indicate the temperature on a dial on the face of the sterilizer. It does not detect cool air pockets at the center of the load or linen packs.

(2) Recording thermometers indicate and record the same temperatures that indicating thermometers show. They also record the duration of the exposure time for each sterilizing cycle. If exposure periods are greater or less than prescribed, or if the temperature has not been maintained within proper limits, there is a positive record of the errors, thus providing necessary information upon which to act

in correcting discrepancies. The records of the recorder should contain the number of the sterilizer, the time, and the date. Recording thermometers, like indicating thermometers, do not detect cool air pockets.

b. Thermal indicators are used to detect conditions inside the sterilizer chamber. They are useful for checking packaging and loading techniques as well as exposure to sterilizing cycles. THERMAL INDICATORS DETECT OPERATOR MISTAKES AND/OR STERILIZER MALFUNCTION BUT THEY DO NOT "PROVE" STERILIZATION. The two most widely used types of thermal indicators are:

(1) Heat-sensitive tape that has lines or squares that turn dark when the package is exposed to heat and certain conditions of time and temperature are met. This tape is not a check on the sterility of the package. Its primary function is to indicate that the package has been exposed to a sterilizing cycle.

(2) A sealed glass tube containing a small tablet which melts when certain conditions of heat and temperature are met and maintained for a specified period of time. These tubes are placed at the center of packages as they are wrapped. If the tablet has not melted when the package is opened, then the package has not been exposed to sterilizing conditions.

c. The Bowie-Dick test measures the adequacy of residual air removal and the uniformity of steam penetration in the prevacuum, high-temperature sterilizer. Commercial test sheets or a piece of fabric with 4 or 5, 8-inch strips of heat-sensitive tape crisscrossed on the surface, may be used for the test. The test must be performed daily:

(1) Place the test sheet or fabric in the center of a linen pack and process this single pack through the sterilizing cycle.

(2) Remove the test sheet or fabric from the pack and examine the markings for color change. If the color change is uniform (all lines or circles darkened) it suggests that the sterilizer is functioning properly.

(3) Irregular color changes suggest the presence of residual air in and faulty operation of the sterilizer.

(4) If the prevacuum, high-temperature sterilizer cannot pass the Bowie-Dick test, it should be considered a gravity displacement sterilizer and operated as such.

d. Biological indicators are used to check sterilization efficiency. Negative reports from biological controls prove that wrapping techniques are correct and that the sterilizer is working properly for the load that is being tested. Tests should be conducted once a week, but more frequent testing may be necessary under adverse conditions or when sterilizers are old or troublesome. Commercially prepared spore strips using highly resistant spores in known populations are used to check sterilizer efficiency. Spore strips containing *B. subtilis* are used to check ethylene oxide sterilizers and *B. stearothermophilus* is the organism of choice to check steam sterilizers:

(1) In checking the steam sterilizer, the spore strips are placed in the center of a large linen pack, which is then placed in the front, bottom position of the sterilizer (the position most likely to retain trapped air).

(2) In checking the ethylene oxide sterilizer, the spore strips are placed in various areas throughout the load as well as inside of packaged items.

(3) Following exposure to the sterilizing cycle, the spore strips are sent to a bacteriology laboratory for determination of results. If a bacteriology laboratory is not available locally, the spore strips may be sent to a commercial laboratory or to the manufacturer of the spore strips.

e. If any of the foregoing indicators shows erratic sterilizer operation, trained maintenance personnel should check the sterilizer at once.

13. Steam Sterilizer Maintenance. In order to keep these sterilizers in proper working order, they must be cleaned and inspected regularly. Daily and weekly routines should be established as follows:

a. The interior of the chamber and the chamber drain strainer should be cleaned daily. This cleaning should be done in the morning when the sterilizer is cool:

(1) Wash the inside of the chamber, the door, and all trays, carriages, and racks with a mild detergent and rinse well with plain water. Strong abrasives, steel wool, or similar substances must not be used as they can damage surface areas.

(2) Remove the chamber drain strainer and use a brush to clean lint and sediment from its pores. If the strainer is not kept clean, the sterilizer cannot be depended upon for sterilization.

b. The chamber discharge line and trap should be flushed once a week. Remove the strainer and flush the chamber drain line with a hot solution consisting of 1 ounce of trisodium phosphate to 1 quart of water or use a nonphosphate detergent as a flushing agent. Then flush the line with 1 quart of plain hot water and replace the strainer.

c. Qualified maintenance personnel should inspect and maintain the sterilizers regularly to protect them from superheated (unsaturated) steam, incomplete air exhaustion, and other factors resulting from mechanical failure.

SECTION C—PROCESSING SUPPLIES FOR STERILIZATION

14. Introduction. Specific items which are processed and sterilized in the surgical suite will be determined by local policies, the surgical specialties available, and the extent to which disposable products are used. These items will usually include, but are not limited to, instruments and instrument sets, utensils, linens, and fluids.

15. Cleaning, Sorting, and Inspecting. Instruments, utensils, and similar items must be thoroughly cleaned prior to being processed for sterilization. All foreign material must be removed in order for the sterilizing agent to come in direct contact with the surfaces of the object to be sterilized. For linens the "cleaning" is done by laundering and is accomplished through linen supply. Following thorough cleaning and drying, all items must be sorted, inspected, and tested. Like items should be placed together.

  a. Inspect all metal items for signs of rust, cracks, chips, bent areas, or missing pieces.

  b. Check jointed instruments to assure free movement, full closure, and locking of ratchets and to assure that the teeth or serrations meet properly.

  c. Check sharp or pointed instruments for sharp edges or points and, if applicable, proper closure of cutting edges.

  d. Spinal needles and others requiring a stylet should be sorted according to type, gauge, and length. The needle and its corresponding stylet should be straight, sharp, and free from hooks and burrs.

  e. Sort suture needles according to type and size and inspect them for burrs, hooks, dullness or distortion from normal shape.

  f. Endoscopy instruments should be checked for scratches or other defects that may appear on the metal. Inspect both the outside and inside of the cannula. Check to assure that the lens cover is not cracked or cloudy and that the bulbs are working. The connectors should be tight and there should be no breaks in the wire insulation.

  g. Linen should be inspected for tears, holes, thin or frayed areas, ripped seams, missing ties or belts, stains or other defects.

  h. Local policy should be followed regarding repair, replacement, or disposal of items which are not serviceable in their present condition.

16. Packaging for Sterilization. Most items must be packaged before they are sterilized so that they will stay sterile until they are ready for use. (This does not apply to instruments sterilized in open trays and taken directly to the operating room or articles sterilized in liquid germicides.) Several types of packaging materials are available. Paper, plastic, and fabric wrappers are commonly used, and they are not necessarily interchangeable. However, all must meet certain prerequisites:

  a. The wrapping material must provide protection against contamination in handling after sterilization.

  b. It must be an effective dust filter and guard against insects and vermin entering when the package is stored.

  c. The wrapping material must be of known porosity and must be permeable to the sterilizing agent.

  d. The wrapper must be durable enough to withstand the handling that is necessary from the time an item is wrapped, through sterilization, storage, and use.

  e. The size, shape, and nature of the item to be packaged must be considered. For example, sharp or pointed items must be packed so that they cannot cut or penetrate the wrapping material.

17. Size and Density of Packages. The size and density of the package to be sterilized have a direct relationship to the time that is required for the sterilization process. Basic exposure times have been established as 30 minutes at 250° F for the gravity displacement sterilizer and 4 minutes at 270° F for the prevacuum high-temperature sterilizer. In order to assure positive steam penetration and sterilization at these times and temperatures, the dimensions of the largest package should not exceed 12 by 12 by 20 inches and 12 pounds in weight.

18. Arranging Items for Packaging. A standard method of arranging items is necessary in order to assemble a package properly. This is usually done by an indexed file-card system. The file card should describe the use, method of cleaning, contents, wrapping, sterilization, storage and stock level. An example of the suggested entries on the index file card is shown in figure 3.

  a. Packages should be wrapped loosely and arranged so that the sterilizing agent will circulate freely into the center of the contents.

  b. Different types of supplies, such as basins and linens, should not be included in the same package for sterilization.

  c. Impermeable surfaces must be separated by a porous material.

> Use: (State the purpose for which this set will be used.)
>
> Contents: (List in detail the items contained in this set.)
>
> Wrapping: (State method for wrapping set.)
>
> Sterilization: (State recommended method or methods for sterilization.)
>
> Storage: (State the storage area for the set, including the cabinet and shelf numbers.)
>
> Level: (Give the number of sets which is considered an adequate level for operations.)
>
> Cleaning: (State the recommended cleaning method or methods for items contained in set.)

Figure 3. Suggested Entries on Index File Card.

d. Box locks on instruments must be open for positive penetration by the sterilizing agent.

e. Items should be arranged in the order or sequence in which they will be used as much as possible.

19. Methods of Wrapping. There are several acceptable ways to wrap packages. The wrapper must be large enough to wrap completely around the item that is to be packaged. Linen wrappers should consist of four thicknesses (two double thicknesses). Two basic methods of wrapping packages are by the diagonal method and the straight method.

a. The diagonal (butcher wrap or envelope style) is used for small packages. Two wrappers should be used, but if only one wrapper is used, or if the second wrapper is used as part of the inner package, the item will have been wrapped in a double-thickness instead of a four-thickness wrapper.

(1) Place two wrappers of the same size, one on top of the other, on the work table with one corner toward you. Place the item to be wrapped in the center of the wrapper, parallel to the table edge.

(2) Fold the nearest corner over the item to be wrapped, then fold the same corner back to the point of the original fold.

(3) Fold the left corner over the item that is being wrapped and then fold the right corner over the item.

(4) Fold the remaining corner toward you and secure without tucking the corner.

b. The straight fold (drug store or square wrap) is used for basin sets and linen packs when sheets are used instead of a wrapper.

(1) Place the item that is to be wrapped in the center of the wrapper and square with its sides.

(2) Fold the side toward you over the top of the item that is being wrapped, and then half-fold it back toward you, making a cuff.

(3) Repeat step (2) with the other side.

(4) Fold the left side over the item that is being wrapped, tucking the ends under the outer fold.

(5) Repeat step (4) with the opposite end.

(6) Secure the package with indicator tape. A linen pack wrapped by the straight fold method is illustrated in figure 4.

20. Labeling Packages. The contents of packs, packages, sets, and fluids must be identified as the supplies are prepared. Otherwise, it would be impossible to know the contents of each pack or the type of fluid once they are all mixed together for sterilization. In addition, each must be dated when it is removed from the sterilizer.

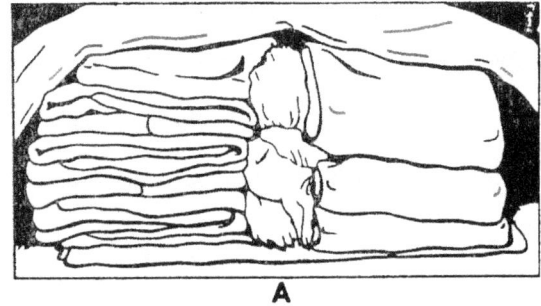

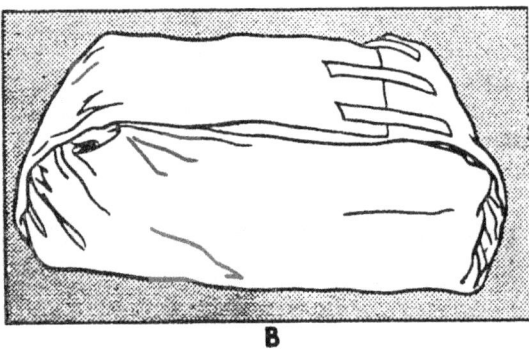

Figure 4. Linen Pack Wrapped by the Straight Fold Method.

a. Information on the label should include the name of the article and the initials of the person preparing the package. Standard nomenclature and abbreviations should be used.

b. Date the packages as they are removed from the sterilizer. (Undated packages are not considered sterile.) The date used is the date when the sterility of the item is no longer assured; that is, the date when the package must be returned for reprocessing.

SECTION D—DISINFECTION

21. Definition. Disinfection is a process which destroys or inhibits the growth of microorganisms, but which cannot be relied upon to produce sterility. Disinfection must be clearly differentiated from sterilization since disinfection may or may not destroy microorganisms, but sterilization completely destroys them.

22. Purpose of Disinfection. Disinfection is used when sterilization is not feasible. Ideally, all material that is used in the care of patients should be sterilized. However, the construction of many materials and the procedures available to sterilize by thermal methods make this impossible. In addition, chemical agents capable of producing sterilization are too toxic for use on human body surfaces.

23. Methods of Disinfection. Disinfection may be accomplished by chemical agents (germicides) or by physical means (boiling):

a. Although some chemical agents are capable of causing sterilization under specific conditions, the use of chemicals normally results only in disinfection.

b. Boiling is the least desirable method of disinfection and should be used only in an emergency or when no other suitable disinfecting agent is available. Boiling is not used for disinfection in hospitals.

24. Antisepsis. Antisepsis is the process of using a mild disinfectant to render the skin and mucous membrane as free of microorganisms as possible. In this case, the relatively weak disinfectant is called an antiseptic. Antisepsis does not produce sterility as most disinfectants capable of destroying microorganisms would also destroy the tissue. (Alcohol is an exception as it is antiseptic and germicidal in the same concentration.)

25. Classifications of Articles for Disinfection. Articles to be disinfected are divided into two general categories: (1) housekeeping, and (2) instruments. Instruments are further subdivided into critical and noncritical categories.

a. Housekeeping disinfection, as the name implies, is disinfection of floors, walls, furniture, and large equipment items.

b. Instrument disinfection is divided into critical and noncritical categories according to the risk of infection involved:

(1) Critical instruments are those used to work beneath body surface areas. This also includes other instruments or items which may be attached to the basic instrument. Instruments classified as "critical" must be sterilized prior to use.

(2) Noncritical instruments are those which do not penetrate body surface areas, so sterilization, while desirable, is not essential.

26. Basic Principles of Chemical Disinfection. Certain basic principles form the basis for all procedures involved in chemical disinfection:

a. The type and resistance of microorganisms determine the effectiveness of a chemical agent.

b. Disinfectants vary in their level of effectiveness according to the chemical agent and the manner in which it is used.

c. Other factors to consider:

(1) The solution must be of sufficient strength to be lethal to the microorganisms for which it is intended.

(2) The entire surface of the item to be disinfected must be exposed to the disinfectant.

(3) The exposure period must be accurately timed as time is important for bactericidal effect.

27. Factors Influencing the Effectiveness of Chemical Disinfection. Several factors influence the effectiveness and efficiency with which a chemical will destroy microorganisms. These factors must be considered when selecting the chemical agent and procedure to be used for disinfecting specific items.

a. All items must be absolutely clean and dry. If the item is not clean, the disinfectant cannot contact the surface and any moisture present will dilute the concentration of the chemical.

b. The number of microorganisms present also affect the performance of a disinfectant. The more microorganisms present, the longer it will take for the germicide to destroy them. This further stresses the necessity for cleaning prior to disinfecting.

c. The type of microorganisms to be dealt with are an important consideration. Most chemical disinfectants can destroy vegetative bacterial forms fairly easily; however, resistant forms, some viruses, and bacterial spores are more difficult to control.

d. The concentration of a chemical agent will determine its effectiveness as a disinfectant. A good germicide, in its use-concentration, should rapidly kill the microorganisms for which it is intended. The germicidal action of some chemical agents can be increased by increasing the concentration of the chemical.

e. Any organic substance such as blood, feces, or tissue will diminish the activity of the chemical. This is an additional reason why everything must be cleaned prior to disinfection.

f. The temperature of the solution will also influence the rate of disinfection. The rate will increase with an increase in temperature and decrease with a decrease in temperature.

28. Procedure for Disinfection. Chemical agents used for disinfection are primarily in liquid form and the articles to be disinfected should be disassembled, if possible.

a. The first step must be a thorough cleaning and drying of the items to be disinfected.

(1) Use cleaning agents selected for the type of material to be cleaned.

(2) Change the cleaning solution frequently. The kind and amount of soil will affect the length of time a cleaning agent will remain active.

(3) Apply friction to remove soil and use brushes to clean tubular instruments.

(4) After cleaning, rinse thoroughly in tap water and follow with a distilled water rinse.

(5) Heat dry items which are not heat sensitive. Place them in the steam sterilizer chamber with the steam off and the door open.

(6) Air-dry heat sensitive items by exposing them to room air.

b. Submerge the clean, dry item in the proper disinfecting solution. Start timing as soon as the item is submerged and remove it from the solution when the specified time has elapsed.

29. Properties of Frequently Used Chemical Disinfectants. The chemical selected to disinfect a specific item should be the best one available for the purpose. It must also be safe to handle and nondestructive to the materials on which it is being used. Table 1 gives recommendations for chemical disinfection and sterilization.

a. The alcohols, ethyl and isopropyl, in use-concentrations of 70 percent to 90 percent are useful as antiseptics. They are rapidly cidal to vegetative bacteria and the tubercle bacillus, but precautions must be taken as they are volatile and flammable. They will also dry and irritate the skin. The disinfecting time varies according to the material to be disinfected and the type of organisms present.

b. Formalin is the aqueous solution of formaldehyde gas. Twenty percent formalin is 8 percent formaldehyde. When diluted with alcohol, its action against the tubercle bacillus is increased. It is sporacidal if the exposure time is at least 12 hours. Formalin should be used at room temperature and loses its effectiveness below 65° F. The solution is irritating to the skin, and the fumes are irritating to the eyes and mucous membrane. Bard Parker solution is a combination of 8 percent formaldehyde and 70 percent alcohol.

c. Glutaraldehyde in a 2 percent aqueous solution (Cidex) is recommended for disinfection of cystoscopes and other lensed instruments. It will destroy tubercle bacillus within a few minutes and spores in 10 hours. The solution is toxic, but the fumes are less irritating than those of formalin.

d. Iodine in the correct concentration is high in germicidal effect and low in tissue toxicity. However, iodine is a staining agent so it is often mixed with a detergent to reduce the staining caused by the iodine. These iodine-detergent combinations are called iodophors. Wescodyne, Hi-sine, Ioclide, Betadine, and Povidone are examples of iodophors. Iodophors with 100 ppm of available iodine are effective in destroying vegetative bacteria, and in higher concentrations, 500 ppm, they are effective

Table 1. Recommendations for Chemical Disinfection and Sterilization

Objects	Disinfection — Category A: Vegetative bacteria and fungi, influenza viruses.	Disinfection — Category B: Category A, plus tubercle bacillus, and enteroviruses.	Sterilization — Categories A & B, plus hepatitis viruses$, bacterial and some fungal spores.
Smooth, hard-surfaced objects	1a - 10 min. 2 - 5 min. 3 - 10 min. 4a - 10 min. 5a - 10 min. 8 - 5 min. 9 - 5 min.	1b - 15 min. 2 - 10 min. 4b - 20 min. 5b - 20 min. 8 - 15 min. 9 - 15 min.	2 - 18 hours 7 - 3 to 12 hours@ 8 - 12 hours 9 - 10 hours
Rubber tubing and catheters#	3 - 10 min. 4a - 10 min. 5a - 5 min.	4b - 20 min. 5b - 20 min. 9 - 15 min.	7 - 3 to 12 hours@
Polyethylene tubing and catheters#	1a - 10 min. 3 - 10 min. 4a - 10 min. 5 - 10 min.	1b - 15 min. 4b - 20 min. 5b - 20 min. 9 - 15 min.	2 - 12 hours 7 - 3 to 12 hours@ 8 - 12 hours 9 - 10 hours
Lensed instruments	3 - 10 min. 4a - 10 min. 5a - 10 min.	8 - 15 min. 9 - 15 min.	7 - 3 to 12 hours@ 8 - 12 hours 9 - 10 hours
Thermometers‡	1c - 10 min.	1c - 15 min.	2 - 12 hours 7 - 3 to 12 hours@ (cold cycle only) 8 - 12 hours 9 - 10 hours
Hinged instrumentsZ	1a - 15 min. 2 - 10 min. 3 - 20 min. 4a - 20 min. 5a - 15 min. 8 - 10 min. 9 - 10 min.	1b - 20 min. 2 - 15 min. 4b - 30 min. 5b - 30 min. 8 - 20 min. 9 - 20 min.	7 - 3 to 12 hours@ 8 - 12 hours 9 - 10 hours
Inhalation anesthesia equipment	1a - 15 min. 3 - 20 min. 9 - 5 min.	1b - 20 min. 9 - 20 min.	7 - 3 to 12 hours@ 9 - 10 hours
Floors, furniture, walls, etc.	3 4a 5a 6a	4b 5b 6b	None

KEY TO AGENTS APPEARING IN TABLE

1a. Ethyl or isopropyl alcohol* (70-90%)
1b. Ethyl alcohol (70-90%)
1c. 1a. + 0.2% iodine
2. Formaldehyde (8%) + alcohol (70%) solution*
3. Quaternary ammonium solutions* (1:500 aq.)
4a. Iodophor - 100 ppm available iodine*
4b. Iodophor - 500 ppm available iodine*
5a. Phenolic solutions (1% aq.)*
5b. Phenolic solutions (2% aq.)*
6a. Sodium hypochlorite, 2000 ppm
6b. Sodium hypochlorite (1%)
7. Ethylene oxide gas
8. Aqueous formalin (20%)
9. Activated glutaraldehyde (2% aq.)

* 0.2% sodium nitrite should be present in alcohols, formalin, formaldehyde-alcohol, quaternary ammonium, and iodophor solutions to prevent corrosion; and 0.5% sodium bicarbonate should be present in phenolic solutions to prevent corrosion.

$ Very little direct observation has been possible.

Be certain tubing is completely filled.

‡ Thermometers must be thoroughly wiped, preferably with soap and water, before disinfection or sterilization. Alcohol-iodine solutions will remove markings on poor-grade thermometers.

@ Depending upon procedure used, more rapidly cidal for category A and B microorganisms.

Z Must first be cleansed grossly free of organic salt.

Germicidal Agent	Chemical Base
Phenol or Carbolic Acid	Creosol
Hexachlorophine	Chlorinated Phenolic
Benzalkonium Chloride (Zephiran)	Quaternary Ammonium
Isopropyl Alcohol	Isopropyl Alcohol
Bard-Parker Solution	Formaldehyde
Staphene and Vesphene	Phenol
Wescodyne	Idophor
Cidex	Glutaraldehyde

against the tubercle bacillus. Iodophors are frequently used as antiseptics because they rapidly degerm the skin and are relatively nontoxic. For some procedures, it is advantageous to use an iodine-alcohol disinfectant. A 1- to 2-percent iodine in 70 percent alcohol is a good antiseptic, and 2 percent iodine in 70 percent to 90 percent alcohol may be used to disinfect thermometers. Iodine solutions are corrosive and 0.2 percent sodium nitrite should be present in the solution to prevent corrosion.

e. Phenol (carbolic acid) is a solution of phenol and phenol derivatives (Creosols). Phenol, as such, is rarely used as a disinfectant. However, many compounds are derived from phenol. Staphene, O-syl, and San Pheno are examples of one percent aqueous phenolic solutions and Vesphine, Tergisyl, and Di-Crobe are two percent phenolic solutions. In the proper concentration these solutions are effective against vegetative bacteria and tubercle bacillus, but they are not effective against spores. These agents in a two percent solution are the agent of choice when dealing with fecal contamination (*E. coli*). Phenolic compounds are stable and remain active after mild heating or prolonged drying. A dry surface previously treated with a phenolic compound, which becomes moist again will become bactericidal. Phenolic compounds irritate the skin and are corrosive. 0.5 percent sodium bicarbonate should be present in phenolic compounds to lessen corrosion.

f. Some of the synthetic cationic detergents containing quaternary ammonium compounds have some germicidal activity. The "quats," in the proper concentrations, are effective in destroying vegetative bacteria but the length of exposure time required limits its usefulness. They are ineffective against the tubercle bacillus and spores and do not inactivate viruses. The "quats" are bland in nature. The "quats" are not good antiseptics as they are inactivated by soaps and detergents. Fabric will absorb the "quats" from a solution and rapidly dilute the concentrations. Zephiran 1:750 is the most commonly used quaternary ammonium disinfectant.

SECTION E—ASEPTIC TECHNIQUE

30. Introduction. Aseptic technique is performance characterized by precautions for constant exclusion of microorganisms. To perform an aseptic procedure means to take the precautions and follow the practices and safeguards which are necessary to create an aseptic condition. A protective barrier is created by wearing gowns, masks, and gloves. Handwashing, disinfection, and sterilization are all methods of excluding or controlling microorganisms.

31. Principles of Aseptic Technique. All personnel must be familiar with and observe the following general principles of aseptic technique:

a. An article is either sterile or nonsterile. IF THERE IS ANY DOUBT, CONSIDER IT NONSTERILE.

b. Touch only the outside of the wrapper or cover when opening a container with ungloved hands.

c. Always open sterile packages and packs away from the body.

d. Do not reach across sterile items unless you are gowned and gloved.

e. Always handle sterile articles with a sterile instrument or sterile gloves.

f. Once an article is removed from a sterile container, do not return it to that container.

g. Always put sterile articles on a dry surface.

h. Do not place sterile articles on the floor.

i. The principles of aseptic technique should be applied when creating and maintaining a sterile field.

j. Cleanliness of the entire work area is basic to sterility. Certain areas of articles are considered unsterile. Tables are sterile only at table level or on their flat working surfaces. Outer rims of the lids of containers, the edges of wrappers, and the rims of flasks are never considered sterile.

k. Once a sterile field has been created, it must be kept sterile until the operation or procedure is finished. Sterile surfaces must touch only a sterile surface. Moisture may contaminate a sterile field; for example, solution basins may spill and soak through covers or drapes. Adhere to all of the principles of aseptic technique. Avoid questionable circumstances, if there is any doubt, consider the item or action as unsterile.

32. Importance of Maintaining Aseptic Technique. Operating room personnel must be acutely aware of the necessity of maintaining aseptic technique throughout all operative procedures. The patient is the loser when aseptic technique is broken. A sterile article does not change appearance if it is touched by an unsterile article, such as a sleeve or hand. However, the item has been contaminated and is capable of transmitting infection. It is always better to replace a contaminated article or setup a new sterile field than to risk causing an infection in the patient.

HEALTHCARE WIDE HAZARDS
GLUTERALDEHYDE

Potential Hazard

Exposure of employees to glutaraldehyde. Glutaraldehyde is a toxic chemical that is used as a cold sterilant to disinfect and clean heat-sensitive medical, surgical and dental equipment. It is found in products such as Cidex, Aldesen, Hospex, Sporicidin, Omnicide, Matricide, Wavicide and others. Glutaraldehyde is also used as a tissue fixative in histology and pathology labs and as a hardening agent in the development of x-rays.

The National Institute for Occupational Safety and Health (NIOSH) suggests ways in which health care workers may be exposed to glutaraldehyde including:
- Hospital staff who work in areas with a cold sterilizing procedure that uses glutaraldehyde (e.g., gastroenterology or cardiology departments).

- Hospital staff who work in operating rooms, dialysis departments, endoscopy units, and intensive care units, where glutaraldehyde formulations are used in infection control procedures.

- Central Supply workers who use glutaraldehyde as a sterilant.

- Research Technicians, researchers, and pharmacy personnel who either prepare the alkaline solutions or fix tissues in histology and pathology labs.

- Laboratory workers who sterilize bench tops with glutaraldehyde solutions.

- Workers who develop x-rays.

Glutaraldehyde is used in a limited number of applications, rather than as a general disinfectant. Specific applications include use as a disinfecting agent for respiratory therapy equipment, bronchoscopes, physical therapy whirlpool tubs, surgical instruments, anesthesia equipment parts, x-ray tabletops, dialyzers, and dialysis treatment equipment (Air contaminants, Section 7 - VII. Feasibility and Regulatory Analyses).

Health effects of glutaraldehyde exposure include:
- **Short term (acute) effects:** Contact with glutaraldehyde liquid and vapor can severely irritate the eyes, and at higher concentrations burns the skin. Breathing glutaraldehyde can irritate the nose, throat, and respiratory tract, causing coughing and wheezing, nausea, headaches, drowsiness, nosebleeds, and dizziness.

- **Long-term (chronic) effects:** Glutaraldehyde is a sensitizer. This means some workers will become very sensitive to glutaraldehyde and have strong reactions if they are exposed to even small amounts. Workers may get sudden asthma attacks with difficult breathing, wheezing, coughing, and tightness in the chest. Prolonged exposure can cause a skin allergy and chronic eczema, and afterwards, exposure to small amounts produces severe itching and skin rashes. It has been implicated as a possible cause of occupational asthma.

Possible Solutions

Limit exposure to glutaraldehyde through work practice, engineering controls and personal protective equipment (PPE) including:
- Make sure that rooms in which glutaraldehyde is to be used are well ventilated and large enough to ensure adequate dilution of vapor, with a minimum air exchange rate of 10 air changes per hour.
    - Ideally, install local exhaust ventilation such as properly functioning laboratory fume hoods (capture velocity of at least 100 feet per minute) to control vapor.
    - Keep glutaraldehyde baths under a fume hood where possible.
- Use only enough glutaraldehyde to perform the required disinfecting procedure.
- Store glutaraldehyde in closed containers in well ventilated areas. Air-tight containers are available. Post signs to remind staff to replace lids after using product.
- Use specially designed, mobile, compact, disinfectant soaking stations to facilitate sterilization of heat sensitive equipment such as endoscopes, or GI scopes. These soaking stations provide an enclosed area for sterilizing trays, and remove fumes from glutaraldehyde and other disinfectants.
- Use appropriate PPE covered under [29 CFR 1910.132(a)] including:
    - Use gloves that are impervious to glutaraldehyde such as those made of Butyl Rubber, Nitrile, and Viton®, which have been shown to provide full shift protection from glutaraldehyde.
    - For shorter exposures, you can use gloves made of polyethylene. Do not use Neoprene and PVC gloves because they do not provide adequate protection against glutaraldehyde and may actually absorb it.
    - Do not use latex surgical exam gloves for skin protection against glutaraldehyde, except in situations where only short-term, incidental contact is expected.
    - Wear lab coats, aprons, or gowns made of appropriate materials such as polypropylene to provide additional protection.
    - Wear splash-proof goggles and/or full face shields when working with glutaraldehyde to protect eyes.
- All employees who may be exposed to above the ceiling threshold limit value (TLV) of 0.05 ppm, should use appropriate respirators for glutaraldehyde vapor during routine or emergency work. Respirator requirements are found in the OSHA respiratory protection standard [29 CFR 1910.134]
- Provide eye wash fountains for immediate emergency use [29 CFR 1910.151(c)].
    - Use eye wash fountains and emergency showers if there is skin contact with glutaraldehyde. Flush area with water for at least 15 minutes to remove chemical.
    - Change into clean clothes if clothing becomes contaminated.
- Clean up spills immediately.
    - Refer to ANSI/AAMI [1996] for further information about emergency procedures in the event of a large spill.
- Do not eat, drink, or smoke in any area where glutaraldehyde is handled or stored.

- Use a vacuum or wet method to reduce dust while cleaning up pure glutaraldehyde. Do not dry sweep.

- Use less toxic products if feasible and available, or other processes for sterilization.

- Automate the transfer of pure glutaraldehyde or pump liquid glutaraldehyde from drums or other storage containers to appropriate containers and operations, avoiding exposure to glutaraldehyde by keeping it in a contained process.

- Hazard Communication Standard [29 CFR 1910.1200] requires employers to ensure that the hazards of all chemicals are evaluated and that this information is transmitted to the employees by means of a hazards communication program which includes, labeling, material safety data sheets, and employee training.

Additional Information:
- Best Practices for the Safe Use of Glutaraldehyde in Health Care [261 KB PDF*, 48 pages]. OSHA Publication 3258-08N, (2006).

- OSHA does not currently have a required permissible exposure level (PEL) for glutaraldehyde.
    - The American Conference of Government Industrial Hygienists (ACGIH) has a recommended ceiling Threshold Limit Value (TLV) of 0.05 ppm (parts per million). This represents an airborne concentration that should not be exceeded during any part of the work shift.
    - NIOSH has established a recommended exposure limit of 0.2 ppm for glutaraldehyde vapor from either activated or unactivated solutions. This TLV is based on the irritation threshold in humans.
- Glutaraldehyde Occupational Hazards in Hospitals. US Department of Health Human Services (DHHS), National Institute for Occupational Safety and Health (NIOSH) Publication No. 2001-115, (2001, May).

- Air Contaminants. OSHA Preamble to Final Rules, (1989).
    - Section 7 - VII. Feasibility and Regulatory Analyses
- Use of Latex Surgical Exam Gloves for Protection Against Glutaraldehyde. OSHA Standard Interpretation, (1997, October 3).

- *American National Standards Institute/ Association for the Advancement of Medical Instrumentation (ANSI/AAMI)*
    - *ST58-1996*, Safe Use and Handling of Glutaraldehyde-based Products in Healthcare Facilities

www.ingramcontent.com/pod-product-compliance
Lightning Source LLC
Chambersburg PA
CBHW081821300426
44116CB00014B/2446